HOW TO LIVE LONGER, HEALTHIER & WEALTHIER

BY

JAYE PURPOSE

CONTENTS

PREFACE

Those who don't know their purpose in life are 2.4x more likely to die sooner than those who do. Yeah...you read that right! That's what the data shows. The closer I got to 30, the more I couldn't stop thinking about why I was here, not in that particular location but on Earth. I kept replaying my 20s in my head.

I was fishing for some remnant of significance in the past 10 years of my life. Where had the time gone? Had I taken full advantage of my time or wasted it? What am I supposed to do going forward? These thoughts are typical of someone approaching a milestone in age.

However, I was determined to find out what I needed to do to ensure I used up the next ten years of my life. I spent a few years obsessed with my *Purpose in Life*. I spent countless hours reading academic journals revolving around psychology, theology, and sociology, opening up 100+ books, and joining calls with experts in the field to seek as much data as possible. I constantly prayed over and meditated upon the most significant questions of life that most people dare not to engage with.

The more I learned, the more astonished I became. My findings were phenomenal. To sum it up, your purpose in life is like a key that unlocks a new life. A longer, healthier, and wealthier life, among many other things. Because of the abundant benefits, I knew this information was something I had to get to other people.

As I discovered my purpose in life, I decided to go back through my journal and create a system for others to follow. The concepts in this book came from all my studies, thoughts, conversations, learning, and testing. If you follow the ideas in this book, you will unlock a life of longevity, health, and wealth!

When I was writing the material for the book, I imagined that *you* reached out to me and asked me to show you how to reveal your purpose in life. After you reached out, we met up and had a sit-down. Everything that I would tell you at that sit down is what came out on the pages you are about to indulge in. So, as you read, just pretend that you and I are sitting comfortably having a casual conversation about one of life's biggest questions.

The conversation is broken down into 3 separate phases: the mindset you need to succeed, the models & frameworks that will help you understand your purpose, and the exercises that will reveal your purpose and the path you should travel. The mindset is the most important thing. Nothing else in the book will work if you don't get that down. For this reason, we'll start with mindset.

PHASE ONE –
The Mindset of Purpose

The first thing you need before you delve into your search is to adopt a few beliefs into your mindset. These 5 principles are essential. Adopting them into your mindset will guarantee success within the framework I am giving you and in life. These principles have stood the test of time and will always hold true. Let's get into it.

CHAPTER 1

THE PRINCIPLES:

The 5 Immutable Principles of Your Life's Purpose

"A mindset is the paradigm through which you experience life. You don't experience life as it is. You experience life as you are."

– Dr. Jamil Sayegh

Have you ever heard of a man named Charles Barkley? Charles Barkley is a retired Hall of Fame basketball player. Known for being one of the toughest guys on the court. He was that guy who would talk trash to you all game long and be willing to get into a fistfight at the drop of a hat. He was one of the best, and he exuded confidence.

But when he got onto a golf course, it was almost like he had become a different person. Charles used to be quite an avid golfer. But his thirst to be great at the game led him to seek advice from anyone he encountered. Through his admission, he stated that he began to be bombarded with different voices as he swung his golf club.

This led to what many know to be the "hiccup" or the "tick" in his golf swing. After receiving advice that a slight pause in his swing would improve his game, he had one of his best days at the golf course. That great day at the golf course made him believe that the "pause" was the one thing that made him a great golfer. He was informed to release the "pause" from his swing as he got better advice. But his belief in this "pause" was so strong he couldn't let it go.

Stuck between a belief he couldn't let go of and a belief he wanted to adopt, the slight pause became an intense hesitation he couldn't release from his game. No matter what evidence appeared, he couldn't shake the belief that the "pause" would make him better. Check out this video to see what eventually became his golf swing.

I know you're thinking, "What does any of this belief business and Sir Barkley have to do with me?" I wanted to show you the power of belief. How could someone be so disciplined, confident, persistent, and ruthless in one sport and the exact opposite in another? That's the power of just one belief. A belief is the most powerful thing on the planet. One belief can make you do things you don't want to do or be the driver to push you towards an object of interest. Now imagine the power a cluster of core beliefs holds over your life.

A mindset is the culmination of deep-seated beliefs that govern your actions. At this very moment, you have an attitude, a set of beliefs, regarding "purpose in life." There are certain beliefs that you have about it. You may be aware of some of them. Others' beliefs may be so suppressed that you are unaware of them. Because beliefs are so powerful, it is paramount that we discuss mindset before we get into any type of strategy regarding our life's purpose.

We'll go over what I call the Principles of Purpose. It's a set of laws concerning purpose that I will propose to you. Whether or not you adopt them into your mindset is up to you. However, if you have a limiting mindset concerning purpose in life, the limitation will create a "hiccup" in your *swing*. After you reveal your purpose, you will inevitably *take a swing* at bringing it to fruition. It doesn't matter how "successful" you are in life. If you've adopted limiting beliefs into your mindset, you will hesitate when taking a swing at it. You will also have a limited view of your purpose in life. So, you must get the correct principles before beginning the revelation!

Asset Vs. Liability?

Is your mind an asset or a liability? Before you decide, let me explain the difference between an asset and a liability. The difference between the two is a matter of a vantage point. A vantage point is a place or position affording a view of something. A liability will place you in a position of disad*vantage*.

In contrast, an asset will place you in a position of ad<u>vantage</u>. An asset will position you one way, and a liability will set you differently. In this sense, it's only a matter of placement.

Two variables I want you to consider are placement and distance. Whenever something is an asset, it will place you in a position free of obstacles. There are no obstacles with assets. Assets are obstacle removers. They create freedom.

Regarding distance, an asset always brings you closer to your desired outcome. All the objects of your desire are but an arm's reach away when your mind is an asset. If this is to be accurate, then the opposite must also be true. A liability must place you in a position surrounded by obstacles. Liabilities are obstacle creators. They create bondage. Concerning distance, liabilities always move you further from your desired outcome. All objects of your desire will be out of your reach when your mind is a liability. This is the difference between the two. Certain words are released from your mouth that indicate the status of your mind.

A mind that is a liability will speak words full of hesitance. Words of hesitance always follow your I's. I don't know, I can't, I won't, I wouldn't, I shouldn't, I might, I don't know, I am not, and even I want are all liabilities. You speak these words all the time without awareness. As you raise your level of awareness, you will catch yourself speaking words that reveal your state of mind. These words show whether your mind is an asset or a liability. They've become a part of your identity and reveal the things you're bound by through speech. A mind that is an asset will speak words of certainty and conviction. Words like I know, I am, I have, and I will are assets. Assets create congruency between the desires and hopes of your spirit and your actions.

Again, is your mind an asset or a liability? Your mind needs to be an asset when you embark on your journey of purpose. The principles you are about to be exposed to can be an asset if you believe them in your heart. Concerning your purpose in life, your mind will be an asset instead of a liability if you adopt these principles.

The wisest man to walk the Earth gave us a proverb that says we must guard our minds because the mind determines the course of our lives. Our mindset determines the course of our entire life. Thus, with purpose, we must be sure to approach it with the right mindset, or all of our attempts to reveal true purpose will be unsuccessful. Understanding the purpose mindset is the most critical part of the process. The purpose mindset has 5 fundamental principles. Here they are.

Coach's Challenge: If you conclude that your mind is a liability, do not be hard on yourself. On the path of turning your mind into an asset, awareness isn't just the first step but also a necessary one. Recognizing that your mindset is a liability doesn't feel good. But in pursuing purpose, you must be vulnerable enough to withstand discomfort.

Before continuing in the book, consider taking me up on a challenge to raise your awareness even higher. Take a sheet of paper and draw a line down the middle. At the top of the left side, title it "assets." At the top of the right side, title it "liabilities." Brainstorm the beliefs in your heart and label them as an asset or liability. Use the description of an asset and a liability in the previous section if you have difficulty giving your beliefs an appropriate label.

Pro tip: If you're struggling with beliefs, note what you've done in the past few days. As you build a list of activities you have done, ask yourself, "What belief is the foundation of this action." Behind every action we take is a belief supporting it. The actions you take are a direct roadmap to the beliefs that live in your heart.

--

Principle #1 — Everything & Everyone Has Purpose

I worked at my dad's cell phone shop when I was around twenty. Sometimes, close friends and family would come to the store and chat. Duke, my brother-in-law, used to come by and hang out from time to time. He would always talk to me about business opportunities. One day, Duke explained how much passive income was generated from his vending machine business. I needed help grasping the concept of passive income and how he knew about this information. I found it hard to believe. It sounded too easy. He was among the first people I ever heard talk about passive income.

Naturally, I started asking tons of questions. My brother-in-law must have felt overwhelmed by my barrage of questions because he stopped me mid-sentence. He enthusiastically looked at me and said, "Just look around the room!" I was utterly lost, but I did it anyway, "ok," I said. He taught me the lesson, "Everything you look at in this room is a business. Business is everywhere. There isn't anything you can lay eyes on that isn't a business. It's all around you. You just have to open your eyes!"

He asked me to follow him outside the store to further his point. We stood about 6 feet from a busy two-way street as we stepped outside. He continued his lesson, "Now look around at all these businesses. There isn't one thing that isn't a business. The material for the streetlight is a business. The lightbulb that produces the light is a business. The cement we're standing on is a business. The fence across the street, the handrail you're leaning against, even the grass across the street are all businesses."

This conversation turned on a lightbulb in my mind. It was one of those moments of enlightenment that I'll never forget. It's a truth that will always hold its validity. If you look around where you are right now, you can't focus on one thing that isn't a business.

Again, you may be thinking, "But what does this have to do with Purpose?" It has everything to do with purpose. The same lesson my brother taught me about business also applies to purpose. Let me give you an excerpt from the story using the word purpose instead of business.

"Just look around the room!" I was utterly lost, but I did it anyway, "ok," I said. He taught me, "Everything you look at in this room has a purpose. Purpose is everywhere. There isn't anything you can lay eyes on that doesn't have purpose. It's all around you. You just have to open your eyes!"

He asked me to follow him outside the store to further his point. We stood about 6 feet from a busy two-way street as we stepped outside. He continued his lesson, "Now look around at all these purposes. There isn't one thing that doesn't have a purpose somewhere. The material for the streetlight has a purpose. The lightbulb that produces the light has a purpose. The cement we're standing on has a purpose. The fence across the street, the handrail you're leaning against, and even the grass across the street all have a purpose."

Do you see the similarities in the stories? The first principle describes the omnipresence of purpose. Purpose is everywhere. Everything has a purpose, and that includes you! To further the point, there are 3 A's of the first principle that provides more detail: All-Around, Accident, and Ahead.

The 3 A's of Principle #1

All-Around

In the same way, that business is all around us, so it is with purpose. It doesn't matter where you are. If you look around, whatever you can lay your eyes on has a purpose. Consider this: we were made in the image of the Creator. Suppose humans have enough sense not to create anything without purpose. Would our Creator not also have enough sense to not create anything without purpose? Unless, of course, you believe that you're wiser than The Creator.

You hold far more importance and potential than anything on Earth. With that being said, because you aren't a mere inanimate object, revealing your purpose in life will be a little more complex. It will take more time and effort. Every member of the human race holds more parts within his being than any inanimate object. You have more than a body. A spirit and a soul live within your body at the core of your existence. This is one of the reasons why your purpose takes more work to reveal.

Nevertheless, purpose is always and always has been all around you. Like I couldn't see all the business around me in my story, many people can't see purpose in their own lives. But just because you haven't seen it with your eyes doesn't mean it doesn't exist. You may need to adjust your eyesight to clarify your purpose.

When you're placed in a position of disadvantage, it's difficult to see things in plain sight. One day, as I was squinting at the TV, my Pop turned and said, "Boy, you always squinting. You probably need some glasses!" With a disgusted look on my face, I responded, "Glasses! I can see just fine. Plus, glasses are for nerds." After a while, he convinced me he needed to take me to an Optometrist to check my eyes. The Optometrist told me my vision was horrible. Within a week, I was walking around with a pair of distinguished frames on my face.

But the crazy thing is what happened after I got my glasses. They placed me in a position of advantage. There were things all around me that I never noticed before. Things that were outside of my limited field of vision. I remember going back to school the day after I got my glasses. That's when I noticed all the things that were in plain sight, but I never saw. The teacher's writing on the board, the projects and infographics along the wall, a friend during passing period walking on the far end of the hallway, the detail on people's faces, and so much more. It was like a whole new world.

The details of your purpose in life are all around you. You just need to be placed at a better vantage point. Your field of vision needs to be opened up. Having the correct principles is like wearing glasses that give you perfect eyesight. You'll be able to see your purpose in life with clarity.

Accident

I've heard several people tell me that they believe their lives hold no purpose. If this were to be accurate, it would mean that you were brought here by accident. We know that everything and everyone has a purpose. This means there are no accidental creations. You are *not* an accident! You did not end up here by happenstance. You are here for a reason.

We've been blessed with the privilege of procreation, recreation, and co-creation. We can do so by utilizing the systems the Creator left behind to meet His original intentions. However, sometimes, someone uses their powers of creation to satisfy ill intentions. When we use the system of creation to meet an ill intent, the original intent will also be satisfied. The original intent is satisfied whether you want it to be or not. We like to wrongfully label the original intent as an accident. In case you are not able to follow, consider this example. There is a system for procreation. When man and woman become one, that system creates a child. That is the original intent of the system.

However, entering that system with the ill intention of self-pleasure is commonplace outside of a covenant relationship. When this happens, the ill intent of self-pleasure is satisfied. Still, the original intent of creating another person is also satisfied. Since the original intent was unwanted, it is often labeled as a *mistake*. It is no accident that the original intent was fulfilled. The fact that your inception met God's original intention does not make you an accident. It makes you a part of royalty. Your existence is enough evidence to prove you weren't accidentally brought here.

Ahead

Purpose always comes ahead of production. There must be a purpose before anything or anyone is brought into production. In other words, purpose will always precede production. Your purpose is older than you are. Without purpose, there is no need for production. This is another way of saying there is no way something could be produced without first having a purpose. The fact that you are reading these words indicates that you have a purpose.

Principle #2 — Purpose is Within

When I began searching for purpose in my life, I looked everywhere. I asked everybody all kinds of questions. I read all the books you could think of. I watched dozens of sermons and other videos. I searched all through my Bible. I prayed about it. The list goes on and on. Needless to say, after all of that, I still felt lost. Until I learned an important truth that put me on the right path toward discovery.

Principle #2 is that purpose is within. Purpose is found internally. It's already inside of you. Many people look for their purpose in life through some external source. External sources are the home of meaning in life.

In contrast, purpose abides in the home of the spirit. This is not meant to degrade the importance of meaning in life. Simply, it's intended to shed light on the differences between meaning and purpose to get you to recognize what is manifesting in your life.

Purpose Vs. Meaning

There are three distinct differences between purpose and meaning.

Reason vs. Result: Purpose is attached to the reason behind something. Meaning is attached to the result of a thing. My grandma used to tell me, "There is a reason for everything!" A reason and a result are attached to time but in different ways. A reason is always connected to a beginning. Reasons are a cause.

In contrast, a result is attached to an ending. If a reason is the cause of something, the result is the effect. The reasons are internal. Results are external. The results we get in life often add the most meaning to our lives. Graduations, birth, marriage, birthdays, etc. are all results. The reasons behind our actions constitute purpose in our lives. To be a success, to be a family, to be in love, to be alive, etc. are all reasons.

He who has a strong enough reason to live can bear almost any how."

– Friedrich Nietzsche

Intention vs. Importance: Purpose is the original intent for creation. Meaning is the significance we attach to an outcome. Think of value. Things that we link more value to always mean more to us. I intend to get a drink because of my thirst. The intention is attached to purpose. It is only as important to me to the degree that I am thirsty. If I were in a desert, the satisfaction of my thirst would *mean* much more to me than if I were at a convenience store with money in my pocket. The greater the intention, the more importance you'll attach to a result.

Fixed vs. Fleeting: Your purpose in life is fixed because it is attached to you. It goes wherever you go. It does not transfer to anyone or anything. Purpose never changes, and it's permanent. Meaning, on the other hand, is fleeting. It doesn't attach itself to you. It comes and goes as it pleases. For example, let's use one of the analogies from above. In the case of graduation, I stated earlier that the purpose for graduating may be to be a *success*. The reason and intention of being a success are fixed.

However, the meaning attached to it is fleeting. Meaning can be attached to anything if the result remains the same. In other words, you can graduate from any school, whether it's Harvard, a community college, or the School of Hard Knocks. As a side note, you will attach different increments of meaning based on how much you trust that graduation will fulfill its purpose of making you a success. But the fact remains that the meaning is attached to *external* objects or circumstances while purpose always lives *internally*.

Internal Vs. External

This is a fascinating dynamic that exists with purpose. That is, it always originates within and manifests in the external world that we live in. Your life's purpose cannot be found anywhere in this 3-dimensional space because it is intrinsic. Your purpose was before you were. It was placed in you when you were brought here to this Earth. It will manifest in the external world, but only after you've discovered it from within.

Meaning, on the other hand, is external and very often manifests internally. It is based on an external object, and its satisfaction provides value inside of you in the form of emotions. Whereas purpose is provided for us and fixed in nature, we attach meaning to things based on our belief systems. We have the power to choose and change what provides meaning for us. This is one of the reasons meaning is fleeting. It is highly emotional, and we are in control of it.

So far, we've covered principle #1, which says everything and everyone has a purpose, and principle #2, which states that purpose is within. Now for principle #3.

Principle #3 — We're already equipped for purpose

Not only does everyone have a purpose for their life, but everyone already has all the resources needed to bring their purpose in life to fruition. We are all equipped to reveal and personify our life's purpose. To be able to live on purpose.

If you buy a finished product, it will have all it needs to function according to its original intent. There will be occasions when you make a purchase, and the product will say, "Batteries not included." So sometimes it won't come with its power source. But guess what? We all came equipped with our very own power source.

That power source is our energy! Energy and other resources were given to us as a gift. A gift that we can and should use to live out our life's purpose. You already have everything you need. It's just a matter of understanding and using your resources.

The Resources

Six primary resources contribute to all things. If you are reading this content, you have every one of these resources to varying degrees. The only difference between you and those you see as successful is how you manage these six resources. The resources are divided into two different components. The first component is you. You are broken down into the body, mind, and spirit. The second component is everything outside of you. This is broken down into matter, space, and time.

Mind, Body & Spirit

Mind, body, and spirit are what makeup who you are. These three aspects of your identity are the governing factors of your life. Each component of who you are comes with different tools for its use. Even if you've never realized it, these three come with all the resources you could ever need. You have to be willing to look deeper than you're used to.

Tools of the Spirit

Your spirit is the true essence of who you are. A culmination of the invisible qualities that make you who you are. This is your most authentic form. There are several tools that the spirit uses to operate. There is intuition, conscience, beliefs, subconscious, and attitude.

Intuition – A strong feeling of conviction without conscious reasoning.

We've all heard of intuition at some point in our lives. It shows up as a hunch or a flash in the mind that reveals the Truth of a matter. Your intuition is a gut feeling. It's a strong feeling that you shouldn't go there or talk to that person. A conviction that a job isn't for you or she isn't the one you should marry. It is a certainty and conviction about a thing that comes *without* the awareness of a logical explanation.

You know something is wrong or right sometimes, but there is no external evidence to prove it. At least none that you know of. All you have to back it up with is the internal conviction within. Frequently, American society refers to it as a *Mother's Intuition*. But this tool isn't reserved for mothers. It is available for anyone who develops the awareness and skill to listen to it.

Conscience – The voice of your spirit and the megaphone of your thoughts & beliefs.

Have you ever wondered why you have two voices? A voice that other humans can hear and another that only you and God can listen to. You could be screaming in your mind, and nobody else could have a clue. Your physical voice belongs to your body, but your conscience is the inner voice that belongs to your spirit. Its familiar tone can only bellow the words of the beliefs that you plant into your subconscious.

The conscience is a valuable tool, but it can also be dangerous. If you haven't planted seeds of Truth into your subconscious, your conscience will attempt to steer you into the land of falsehood. A land that is full of darkness, malice, and confusion. The conscience will scream lies at you, while the light tug of the intuition pulls at your heartstrings. The conscience usually wins because intuition requires awareness and discipline to recognize its warnings.

This is where the adage of having an angel and a demon in the mind waging war on your thoughts comes from. This does not mean that the conscience is demonic. It implies that you and I can allow lies to enter our hearts. When that happens, the conscience will speak accordingly.

Beliefs – A settled or chosen perspective. Acceptance that a thought is Truth.

Beliefs are the most powerful things on Earth. They can move people to do some of the best or worst things. It is easy to look at someone else's life and place judgment without knowing why they believe what they believe. All you see is the action.

But it is the belief that drives everything in our world. A belief is the acceptance of a perspective or a thought as Truth. It is the imprint upon the subconscious that what you see is how the world works. A belief can make you do *anything*. The belief doesn't have to be true. A belief only has to be true to you for it to take over your mind and, eventually, your life.

A belief is what caused the Holocaust. But it was also a belief that caused the Civil Rights Movement. A belief that caused every war that has occurred. Every wedding has happened because of a belief. You go to a particular grocery store because of a belief. When you clock in at work, you do so because of a belief. *Every action is only possible because of the beliefs that live in the heart.*

Beliefs come from hearing. Even if you see something with your eyes, it still *speaks to your mind*. The conscience is always speaking. A recent study done at Queens University by Julie Tseng and Jordan Poppenk revealed that the average adult has just over 6,000 thoughts per day[13]. There is constant chatter being heard in the mind. You are constantly being influenced by endless stimuli in our external world, especially with today's technological advances.

Beliefs can cause flight or bondage. Of the thousands of thoughts you have daily, not every thought becomes a belief. Only the ones we attach to. When we attach to a particular thought, idea, or notion, it becomes a belief. Beliefs are your number one tool and hold enough power to do anything. If you have strong beliefs based upon Truth, you will be limitless.

Subconscious – *The subconscious is to the spirit what the brain is to the body.*

The subconscious is the internal motherboard that guides and directs all thoughts, feelings, and actions. Also, the storehouse for all beliefs & core beliefs. All these elements add up to make your subconscious. Pay attention to the makeup of the word sub-conscious. Sub means below, and conscious means awareness. The subconscious works *below* our *awareness*. Meaning that you have no clue that the subconscious is at work. Unless, of course, you make a valiant effort to raise your awareness.

I always thought that algorithms were only for geniuses. While *creating* an algorithm may be designated for the mathematically gifted, *understanding* how one works is easy. An *algorithm is simply a set of rules* to be followed by a computer. Your phone has an algorithm that tells it what to do under seemingly a million different circumstances.

For example, when you touch the home button, the phone automatically goes to the home screen. You don't know why or how it does it, but it does. The phone has been programmed with laws that it must follow. That's how an algorithm works. Your subconscious works similarly to an algorithm. The beliefs you choose to adopt make up the *algorithm* that the subconscious follows.

Like the phone example, when someone presses one of your *buttons*, the subconscious reads your algorithm. It sends signals so that the mind and body act accordingly. Neuroscientists call this automaticity. When something becomes automatic, it takes root in your subconscious.

Mindset

A mindset is the paradigm through which you experience life. The total of all your beliefs. It is your mindset. A mindset and an attitude are the same. It's made up of a cluster of beliefs. If one belief is powerful enough to control you, imagine what a set of beliefs can do! Each belief comes with information and emotions that generate a particular perception.

Your mindset is the algorithm that your subconscious uses to operate. It's the set of laws that has to be followed. Except it isn't a computer following the orders; it's you. The good news is you get to choose your attitude. You do so by selecting your beliefs. As they add up, they will form your attitude, mindset, paradigm, or whichever you prefer to call it.

The Tools of the Mind

The mind is the mediator between the spirit and the body. It serves as the connector between the two. The mind also has its own set of tools given to you as a set of resources. The mind consists of the intellect, emotions, thoughts, imagination, consciousness, and free will.

Intellect – A person's mental power to reason and understand.

Your intellect is your ability to understand. Commonly grown through the faculties of problem-solving and the attainment and implementation of knowledge. Essentially, your intellect is the storehouse for wisdom. Wisdom is one of the most precious things in the world. Often, a strong intellect grounded through the continual practice of Truth can be the governor of wild emotions.

Emotions – A strong feeling.

Emotions are like the elements. Graceful, beautiful, and beneficial. But when the elements lose control, their effects can be catastrophic. Emotions are intertwined with feelings. There is a vast array of emotions. However, they exist to get you to *move*.

If you look closely, you will notice the word *motion* within the word emotion. It is a Latin term that means to move. Our feelings were a gift to get us to move in a particular direction. If you can gain control of your emotions, you can gain control of your actions and, ultimately, your life.

Thoughts - The mental formation and representation of an idea, opinion, hope, intention, or belief.

As I previously mentioned, our thoughts are numerous. They come from everywhere. Sometimes they serve us, and sometimes they distract us. As I've stated before, thoughts that we attach to become beliefs. When we cling to a thought, it will make an imprint upon our subconscious. This means it will also be added to our attitude.

Because of this, thoughts that continually appear in the mind are the work of the subconscious to prove our beliefs to be true. Again, this doesn't mean the belief is based upon Truth. Only that the subconscious is looking to prove the belief to be true.

Thoughts that come and go usually belong to others. We have the choice to keep them or reject them. At this very moment, you are reading my thoughts. My thoughts are full of words being planted into your mind in the form of thoughts. It is your choice to adopt them or let them go.

This happens every day when you talk to someone, flip on the TV, unlock your phone, check your email, etc. Thoughts are everywhere. You are constantly being fed thoughts that attempt to attach to your heart.

Imagination

The mental faculty that creatively gives shape, form, action, and ultimately life to all desires, plans, and concepts. The TV set for thoughts. The imagination is the play station of the mind. It is where dreams come to life, and we give visions detail. The imagination is like a movie theatre but in your mind. It's always painting motion pictures.

If you take the initiative to choose what you play in your internal movie theater, your life will change dramatically. Also, your imagination is not bound by time. The imagination can go to the past, or it can go to the future. It also is not bound by space. It holds no limits except the ones we place upon it.

Conscious – Awareness (or lack thereof) and response to internal & external environment.

Your consciousness is your level of awareness of your internal and external environment. Your consciousness is like a muscle that can be developed. The more your consciousness grows, the more you will increase your capacity to respond to what happens in your environment.

As the old saying goes, "out of sight of mind." That applies to your internal eyes and your external eyes. If something is outside your level of awareness, you cannot change its influence upon you.

Free Will

Your free will is the power of choice. Everyone has a will. Everyone also exercises their will differently. However, it is a vital tool. A tool that can be used to exercise evil or good. Nevertheless, it's a tool of your mind that everyone has access to.

Tools of The Body

The body is the physical covering you are familiar with and can see. It houses the spirit and the mind and comprises bodily systems and members. The body is a fascinating tool. It has several systems that work interdependently. Each system is like its own world. The body adapts, grows, shrinks, stretches, and even heals itself (within reason). Its tools are its bodily members and energy.

Energy - A Person's Physical and mental Powers (The right to give orders, make decisions, and enforce obedience).

The strength and vitality required for sustained physical or mental activity. Energy is a gift. The only time your energy isn't being depleted is when you sleep and when you operate in your area of gifting. Other than these two circumstances, your energy is constantly being consumed.

Our energy is the physical and mental power used to give orders, make decisions, and enforce obedience. Energy is used to produce action. Energy needs to be protected. Some activities drain your energy more than others. Some people drain your energy more than others. Even some environments will drain your energy more readily than others. You must be a vigilant guard over your energy because energy is needed for action. Faith without works is dead.

Bodily Members – Hands, Feet, Mouth, Ears, Eyes

5 Senses – Hearing, Seeing, Feeling, Tasting, Touching

Our bodily members are the tools we use to influence matter. I find the members to be an odd thing. Because while they are helpful, several people function at extremely high levels of life without them.

Have you ever heard of Nick Vujicic? For years, he was considered the #1 motivational speaker in the world. He is a successful entrepreneur, coach, and a New York Times bestselling author. He has a lovely wife and four beautiful children! He has the level of life that many people only dream of having. He has done all of this, and much more, without limbs. He has no arms or legs. Has this stopped him?! Absolutely not!

There are countless examples of people who lack one or more of the five senses or bodily members, and they are some of the most amazing people. Of all of the resources, these are the least needed.

Time, Space & Matter

Everyone has three external resources: time, space, and matter. They are all representations of pure potential in different forms. Each resource holds potential you can access along your journey of revealing and embodying your purpose in life.

Time – The indefinite progress of existence.

Time is the indefinite progress of existence. It manifests in the form of the past, present, and future. The past is used for learning. The present is to be used for implementation. The future is used for planning change.

Time also comes with inherent seasons. Seasons of change. Life's winters, springs, summers, and falls are in a never-ending cycle. Thank God for the *changing* characteristic of time that we exist in. Without change, every mistake we make would live in eternity. Change allows the opportunity for adjustment and growth. Therefore, time presents the potential for the expansion of Self.

Time exists for you to have the ability to *become* who you were meant to be. Everyone is allotted a certain amount of time. No one knows how much time they are given. Only that every moment must not be taken for granted.

Space – The height, width, and depth dimensions within which all things exist.

Space is another form of pure potential. The world we live in is full of space. Internally, we also have space that is waiting to be tapped into. Internally, space is consumed by beliefs, thoughts, purpose, and all the other invisible traits that make us who we are. We can empty that internal space and fill it with new beliefs and thoughts.

Externally, we consume space with the manifestation of the objects of our minds. Space is the area where action takes place. It is where faith is displayed. That is why people who create at high levels are entitled to more space. They take action upon the ideas and concepts that consume their internal space. That action then creates more room in the physical realm. They often make more money, have more land, know more people, etc. This is the *space* their actions are afforded in the physical world. This creates more space in their internal world for more ideas, Truth, thoughts, etc. It becomes a revolving door. This is what the wisest man to ever walk the planet meant by, "Your gifts shall make room for you."

When you use your gifts, you are rewarded with more *room*. You are afforded more space internally and externally. There is plenty of potential in space. Your potential sits dormant, waiting for you to act within the space you already have by using your gifts. Then more space will be given to you. We will discuss space more in the next chapter, "The Dimensions of Purpose."

Matter

Matter is composed of the physical substances that occupy and move within space. That goes for the visible and invisible aspects of matter. It is all meant to serve as a resource to keep order in the world. There is also a ton of potential to be tapped into in this realm. The cell phone was here at the beginning of time. The internet was already here millennia ago. It's just that nobody had yet tapped into that area of potential within the resource of matter.

Matter is also the physical representation of all the things that exist in our minds. This is also a resource that consumes many people. Not realizing that what we have directly results from what we have done. Even further, what we have done directly results from who we have become. It all begins internally and manifests externally. This is what The Great Teacher meant: "Seek ye first the Kingdom of God and his righteousness, and these things shall be added unto you!"

Remember that you have everything you need to get the job done. These 6 resources constitute everything you need for your purpose in life. Nothing has been done without a combination of these resources. You already have the tools. You just have to tap into them. These make up the foundation that any other resource you may need comes from. If you utilize these resources appropriately, everything else will come to you.

Let's review. Principle number one told us that everything and everyone has a purpose. Principle number two states that purpose is within. The third principle is that you already have the resources to step into your purpose in life. The fourth principle says purpose is the foundation of plans.

Principle #4 — Purpose is the foundation of plans

Have you ever seen someone put an iPad in a dishwasher? I once read a story about a young woman who bought her father an iPad for Christmas. As he opened the gift on Christmas day, he was delighted. He warmly embraced his daughter and thanked her for being so thoughtful as he thought of the many ways he could use the iPad. A few weeks later, the young woman called her father and asked how he liked the iPad. She also asked him if he needed help setting it up and using it. Without hesitation, he informed her that he'd been using it with no problems.

The young woman typically visited her parents at least once per month. It was about that time. So, a few weeks later, she stopped by her parents' house for a visit. As her mother opened the door, she stated, "Your father is in the kitchen using that iPad you bought him! He's been using that thing non-stop since you got it for him." Delighted to have picked out such a good gift for her father, the young woman walked to the kitchen to greet her dad. As she entered the kitchen, she was shocked to find her dad using the iPad as a cutting board to chop vegetables.

As she stood speechless, her father rinsed off the iPad and placed it in the dishwasher rack. Looking up, he noticed his daughter's flushed face and exclaimed, "What's wrong, honey?!"

This story is an excellent example of what happens when you make plans for your life without first seeking and revealing purpose. That is why purpose is the foundation for all plans. Just because you don't know the purpose of your life, it doesn't eliminate the purpose of your life. And sometimes, you may *think* you know what it is but need help understanding. At the end of the book, I'll give you a system called The Filtration System that will give you confidence in what you've revealed as your purpose in life. This way, you don't end up like the father in the story.

When you make plans without knowing what your purpose in life is, you always end up with one of the three forbidden uses. You'll end up wrongfully using your resources and, ultimately, your life. Only plan on using something if you have the foundation of *true* purpose. Ignorance of purpose plus action will always equal one of the three forbidden uses: misuse, abuse, or no use.

The Three Forbidden Uses

Misuse – To Use something for the wrong purpose.

To misuse your life is to use your life and resources for the wrong purpose. Similar to the story I used earlier, it is an excellent example of misuse. Misuse doesn't have to be malicious. More than likely, misuse occurred because of confusion about a good thing instead of the *right* thing. While it could be frowned upon, there is nothing inherently wrong with chopping vegetables on an iPad. There are no immoral, unethical, or malicious implications about wanting chopped vegetables.

However, completely ignoring the original intent of an iPad and instead using it as a cutting board qualifies as *misuse*. Where there is ignorance of purpose, there is also a high likelihood of misuse of your life. When you don't know the right thing to do, all good things become attractive. Purpose is what sheds light on the *right* thing.

Abuse – To Use something for an evil or perverted purpose.

Abuse is the perverted use of your life. When immoral and unethical intentions enter the heart of the mind void of purpose, that life and its resources become abused. There are times when the boundaries of morality and taboo become blurred because of past trauma or erroneous experiences. Ultimately, these situations have a high probability of creating belief in falsehood.

These types of beliefs create distorted views of how reality operates. Remember that a belief is powerful enough to make you do *anything*, no matter how grotesque it may seem to other people. This is why you must guard your heart! When falsehood is mixed with ignorance of purpose, abuse always follows.

Unused – Never having been used or untouched.

It has been said that the graveyard is one of the wealthiest places on Earth because it is full of unused ideas, gifts, and purposes. The third forbidden use is for life to go unused. Emotions are what usually gets in the way of a life that goes unused. Someone who is paralyzed by fear will allow their life to waste away day by day. Not knowing their purpose prevents them from doing anything out of fear that they will go in the wrong direction. This is the boat that many people find themselves floating around in.

Consumed by fear, all your gifts and resources go unused. Stuck using the lower levels of their resources for someone else's gain, courage never makes an appearance in their life. You may ask, "How can my life be unused if I am alive?"

Just because you are moving and breathing is no indicator that you are *alive!* Many people move about in a zombie-like state, having no purpose in life and merely responding to the basic emotions that seek to sustain homeostasis. When you lack knowledge of your purpose in life, you can easily pass through life while your true Self lies dormant, waiting to be unveiled.

So far, we've covered 4 of the 5 purposes. Let's get into the final principle.

Principle #5 — The Purpose of all mankind is to serve

Do you agree that everybody is here to serve? I do, too, but service is the most general sense of our purpose. At its very core, the purpose of humanity is to provide order. Let me explain. I'll start at the top!

What does it mean to serve? What if I told you, "The greatest among you shall be your servant"? How does that make you feel? Do you withdraw at the very word *servant*? When we think of the word servant, we've been programmed to think of someone who moves at the beck and call of some tyrant. A butler, slave, flunkey, or attendant may be some images that pop into your mind. But is that what it means to be a servant?

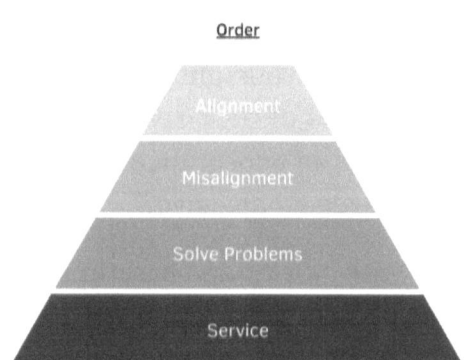

Can you think of any instance where someone is served without the service solving a problem? What it means to be a servant is to be a problem solver or, better yet, a solution supplier. In the example mentioned earlier, the tyrant never calls upon the servant unless he has a problem that must be solved. The same rule applies in everyday life. You can only serve if there's a problem. We hear this in the marketplace all the time. You have to solve problems. You need to know what problem you solve! But how do we solve problems?

Let's start by finding out what a problem is. A problem is an unwelcome or harmful situation. But what makes a situation unwelcome or harmful? Misalignment between a person's desire or needs and their current situation. Misalignment between these two things is the root of any problem.

You will find this to be true if you look at practically anything in life. All things were created out of a problem. The Wright brothers wanted to fly. They couldn't fly, so the misalignment created a problem. It just happened to evoke them enough that they acted on it. Steve Jobs wanted to listen to music without a limited number of songs and the skipping of songs that the compact disc offered. The misalignment created a problem. It moved him enough that he took the steps to create the iPod. This is how everything came into being, including you and me.

You see, misalignment creates issues on every level, not just physically. Think about this! Our body requires that things be kept within certain levels to maintain a state of homeostasis. When our levels go outside these stable levels, it creates a *misalignment* between the body's needs and the current state. This, my friends, creates what we call a P–R–O–B–L–E–M.

Here's an example: if someone's blood pressure is *high*, it creates a misalignment between what the body needs and what is. This misalignment can create all sorts of problems within the body, such as diabetes, heart disease, stroke, aneurysms, and so forth. That's just one example. However, there are endless examples of this, even down to microscopic levels.

So, what is the true meaning of life? Let's start at the top again. The true meaning of life is to serve. But to serve means to solve problems. Even more at its foundation, a problem is just a *mis*alignment. Therefore, to solve any problem means to retain, restore, or reveal natural *alignment*.

Now, to get to the foundation of serving or being a servant, you must answer this one last question. What is alignment? Alignment is order.

So again, at the most general level, we were brought here to serve. But, at the heart of service lies proper order. There is a massive significance in viewing the true meaning of life this way. This perspective is a tremendous help in revealing your purpose in life. Because it is much easier to spot something that is out of order than to spot something that is in service.

When something is out of order, it is automatically a problem. However, if something is in service, it's automatically serving solutions. It's much easier to spot a problem than a solution. If a piece of machinery goes out of service, we usually place a sign in big, bold letters that say, "OUT OF ORDER." If you can't notice that, we have another issue on our hands!

We also use *order* and *service* together quite often. For example, you'll get seated if you go to a restaurant. Then some stranger comes over to you, and they already know why you are there! This stranger is often called a waiter/waitress but also a *server*. The server asks us, would you like something to drink? When they return, we tell them, "I think I am ready to order."... We give the *server* our *order*. The *server* then brings our *order* to us.

Suppose our *order* needs to be appropriately arranged (meaning they brought out the wrong order). In that case, the *server* will take the *order* back and re-*order* the food. The *server* then brings out the food in the correct *order*, and the solution the *server serves* restores the alignment between our hunger and our present state. You went into the restaurant for alignment...or, in other words, order.

Watch this: who has more power, the person serving or the person being served? Listen, the servant always has more power. Why? Because they have access to the source that solves the problem. Whoever has access to the resource always has more power. That is why the greatest person among you is always the servant. The servant has access to the thing that creates order!

One last point about order. There's another word that we sometimes use in conjunction with order. If something was out of order and you saw someone going to use it, what might we say? We would say it doesn't work! Why is this significant? Because the very first order God gave man was to "work."

Before he made man, the Bible says God hadn't yet allowed it to rain because there was no man to "work" the ground. If you go to the first chapter of the Bible, you'll see how he wanted us to work. In the beginning, God told us to be fruitful, multiply, replenish, subdue, and have dominion! What does it mean to have dominion? Dominion is the territory of a sovereign (ruler or a king) or a government. To govern meant to conduct policy, action, and affairs with authority. That word authority means to be able to enforce commands, demand obedience, or give orders!

Recall that I said in principle #1 that purpose always precedes production. But there is no purpose without a problem. Now, many people often search for and look for purpose! But remember, earlier, I also said it's always easier to find a problem than a solution. This equation is another reason why it's better to look for the problem. Because the purpose of production is always equivalent to the inverse of the problem.

So, if the purpose of all mankind lies within order, we have to examine this order thing a little more. Humans can provide order in 3 distinct ways. We can retain, restore, and reveal order. We're the only beings on the planet that can do all three. In the beginning, God created and established order. He then gave us the power to manipulate that order so it could be kept.

Order – The Ultimate Purpose of Life

Order is the foundation of all purposes. Every purpose under the sun functions within one of the three types of order. This means that everyone is here to provide order. The biggest question that leaves is, "How am I supposed to do that?"

That's what we'll answer by the time we get to the end of the book. You will learn the unique ways that you are meant to bring order into the world. This will be your area of service. Knowing this will exponentially increase meaning in your life. Because your level of service will always dictate your level of meaning in life. Remember, the greatest is always the person who serves the most.

Retain - Conserve order (maintain)

Order can be retained by maintaining the natural order established in the beginning. A great example of this is working a 9-5 job. Someone else established order within their domain and needed help retaining that order. This requires little effort. Everything is already set out for you; you just have to not break it.

Restore - Contribute to order (Improve)

We can also restore order that has been ruined. Think of MLK. He did his best to restore the natural order after it was ruined.

Reveal – Create order (Invent)

At the highest level, order can be revealed. At the beginning of time, were there airplanes? Maybe not physically, but were all the resources needed to build a plane on Earth? If so, was the first person to build a plane creating an airplane, or was he revealing what already existed through his faith?

> **Coach's Challenge:** Before diving into the remaining chapters, I encourage you to pause momentarily. Examine the five principles to see if you are working for or against them. Also, do two things before going on 1) Commit the five principles to memory so they shall always be but a thought away, and 2) Re-read the five principles and take notes regarding the thoughts and ideas that enter your mind as you read.

Chapter 1 Summary:

- One of the most essential items in your possession is your mindset—the culmination of deep-seated beliefs that govern actions. Reflect on your current mindset. Is it serving you or holding you back? Beliefs are powerful, and adopting the correct principles is essential for a successful and fulfilling journey toward discovering and realizing one's life purpose.

- The five principles discussed below are potential assets capable of transforming the mind into a positive force for achieving purpose. This is why we all must guard our minds, as it determines the course of one's entire life. *The purpose mindset*, consisting of the five fundamental principles, is an asset that must be deliberately sought after. If not, you will be your worst enemy and the very being that thwarts happiness and purpose.

- *The Five Immutable Principles:*

  - Principle #1: *Everything and everyone has a purpose.* Both business & purpose have an omnipresence about them. Purpose is *all around*, eliminates *accidents*, and comes *ahead* of anything produced.

  - Principle #2: *Purpose is an internal force* that already lives within you. Purpose and meaning often need clarification. While both are significant, they have different characteristics. Purpose is attached to reasons and intentions and is permanent. Meaning is tied to results and importance and is fleeting. The internal nature of purpose contrasts with the external manifestation of meaning.

- Principle #3: *We're already equipped for purpose.* Not only do you have a purpose, but you're also inherently equipped with all the necessary resources to fulfill it. By understanding and effectively utilizing these resources, we can tap into our full potential and purpose in life. We all have six primary resources divided into two components:

  - Internal: Body, Mind, and Spirit

  - External: Matter, Space, Time

- Principle #4: *Purpose is the Foundation of Plans.* Purpose serves as the foundation for effective life planning. There are severe consequences to going through life without knowing your purpose. This often leads to one of the "Three Forbidden Uses" – misuse, abuse, or no use of resources and, ultimately, life. The three forbidden uses serve as cautionary examples. Always align your plans with your life's *true* purpose.

- Principle #5: *The Purpose of All Mankind is To Serve*, and at its core, service involves providing order. Servitude isn't slavery, but instead problem-solving and solution-serving. As a problem solver, the servant holds more power due to their access to resources that create order. The essence of life is to serve by restoring, retaining, or revealing order in the world.

This concludes the first phase of the framework. At this point, it is time to transition the conversation to understanding your purpose in life.

PHASE TWO –
Understanding Purpose

Now that you've finished phase one, it is time for the next puzzle piece. In phase two, we'll learn all the ins and outs of life's purpose. I'll explain the many characteristics, benefits, and even statistics about your purpose that you may have never considered. A solid understanding will help you to better grasp your purpose when it is time for The Revelation toward the end of the book. This phase will cover four chapters: The Prescription, The Pathways, The Perspectives, and The Potential. Let's get started with the Prescription.

CHAPTER 2

THE PRESCRIPTION:

The Prescription To The Life Of Your Dreams

Would you take a bottle of *magic pills* if I offered them to you? You probably wouldn't. But before you completely shut me down, let me tell you about them. Here are the uses for the pill. Suppose you take this pill once a day. In that case, you will live longer, have *better* memory, sleep, decision-making, problem-solving, reasoning, clearer thoughts, a more functional body, more money, *less* disease, depression, anxiety, and malaise.

You will have side effects of joy, peace, and resilience. You don't need to be any particular age, sex, or race for the pill to work for you. You don't need to be a college graduate, in perfect shape, a certain height, or any other qualifier. Also, the pills come in unlimited quantities. Last but certainly not least, you can have them for *free*.

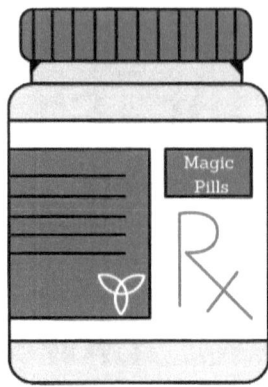

Would you be willing to take the pills now? What if I told you that these pills are real? To be completely honest with you, these pills are real. When you wake up and choose to take every step in stride with your purpose in life, it's the equivalent of taking one of these magic *pills*.

When I started studying the topic of purpose in life, I was shocked to be met by so much data around the topic. There is a study about nearly everything you can think of to determine its relationship with purpose in life. The more I read, the more my curiosity heightened. What I discovered was that your purpose is like a magic pill. It was difficult to digest at first. But the facts were based on experience, not mere theory. I started reading academic journals full of case studies with empirical evidence supporting these claims about purpose. I couldn't believe that this content wasn't more popular.

In this section, I want to highlight some of the material I've encountered that will illuminate some truth. All the things I mentioned about the pill are true. Let's break down a few examples that show exactly what I am talking about. I'll show you a few of the many benefits of living in your purpose: Living longer, Living healthier, Living wealthier, and why you need to start doing it sooner rather than later.

Live Longer

The notion that *"living longer"* is even a possibility could quickly be frowned upon. I'll admit that when I first came across the idea, I thought it was similar to a *pipe dream*. But as I got deeper into the subject of purpose in life, I started finding studies in academic journals performed by sociologists, psychologists, and other professionals. Countless studies exist in the world of academia.

But for those new to the quest for purpose in life, I want you to open your mind as wide as possible before you continue reading. It is easy to dismiss the findings from these studies as *hogwash*. Turn your judgment off for a while and allow yourself to open up to new possibilities.

In 2019, a study titled "Association Between Life Purpose & Mortality among US adults older than 50 years" 3 was done with 6,985 people. The authors used a 7-item test on a 6-point Likert scale to assess the presence of purpose in life. The Likert scale implies that the test wasn't a simple multiple-choice test. Instead, each question posed 6 possible answers ranging from "strongly disagree" to "strongly agree." The authors wanted to find out if there was any correlation between purpose in life and all causes of death.

They also wanted to shed light on life's purpose and any specific causes of death. In other words, does being aware of and living in one's purpose increase, decrease, or have no effect on a person's mortality? That goes for whether death is caused by any specific disease or all diseases. The participants were involved in three rounds of assessments between 2006 and 2010. Unfortunately, during that time, 776 of the participants passed away.

What I want you to understand is that there are a few other studies out there that have had the same intentions as this one. However, this is the only study that assessed psychological effects such as depression, anxiety, clinical hostility, negative affect, and social participation.

In addition, here is a list of sociodemographic and behavioral characteristics included as factors: age, sex, marital status, race, education level, smoking status, functional status, frequency of physical activity, alcohol consumption, presence of chronic conditions, and body mass index.

Here's what that means. The proctors ruled out all of these characteristics in testing. At the end of testing, no one could say any of these traits caused a spike or decrease in the results. Essentially, they considered as many factors as possible to rule out any possible false findings. They analyzed all the data over the four years to assess how the presence of purpose impacted the lives of all the participants.

The findings are astounding. The study revealed that when purpose in life is present in someone's life, mortality is less of a factor. In other words, when you are aware of your purpose in life, you live longer. The study even found other positive traits associated with the presence of purpose in life. We'll get to those in the following few sections.

But in terms of longevity, the study shows that the mortality rate was 2.4 times higher with people who had little or no sense of their purpose in life!! Remember, this is after considering all of the covariates I mentioned earlier. So, for anyone who may be thinking things like, "What about the people who smoke, exercise less than everyone else, or were considered overweight, or any of the other factors that could play into an earlier death?" the discussions are invalid. Even after all of these factors were considered, the result *still* showed a mortality rate that was 2.4 times higher than those who had little or no sense of purpose.

That is *insane*. This means that *when you live your life outside of your purpose, you are 2.4 times more likely to die.* Talk about a wake-up call! Other studies also showed that purpose in a person's life consistently correlated with a lower mortality rate. However, many of them didn't include the covariates that this study did and thus significantly lowered the validity of the results. That's the reason this study was such a big *hit* among academia.

If you're like me, you may be thinking one thing concerning this study. That one thing is age. You may not be 50 or even close to it. In case you missed it, the study I just mentioned is titled "Association Between Life Purpose & Mortality among US Adults Older *than 50 Years!*3" I was curious to know if any other studies with similar objectives also included younger ages.

Luckily, I found another study, Purpose_in Life as a Predictor of Mortality_7, published in 2014. This study included ages ranging from 20-70 years old. The authors followed 7,108 participants over 14 years. They used methods similar to the first study I referenced to assess the presence of purpose in life. The authors included different psychosocial and demographic variables to hold to the study's validity, such as age, sex, race, education, and work status.

Results from this particular study proved that purpose in life promotes greater longevity across all adulthood, not just the older generations. Here's what the authors stated directly, "from a theoretical perspective, we find that endorsing a *strong purpose in life continues to have meaningful reductions in the risk of dying* and that maintaining a stronger purpose in life can be equally important during younger ages as it is at much older ages. Accruing evidence suggests that finding a purpose for your life may add years to it"! The study stresses that purpose in life is associated with a reduced mortality rate in younger ages and the importance of revealing purpose as early as possible.

One drawback of these studies is that they need to show clear causation. There is no clear way to show that purpose is a direct cause of a longer life or that the lack of purpose is a direct cause of a shortened life. We don't know if purpose causes longer life or if the presence of purpose causes better habits that lead to better longevity.

The last thing I want to do is make assumptions. Still, it creates a different lifestyle when purpose is present. A lifestyle that promotes longevity and a decreased mortality rate. Changes in beliefs, self-talk, diet, habits, resource allocation, emotional stability, stress, fitness habits, relationships, and so on reach a higher caliber with the presence of purpose. Regardless of causation, the truth remains that you are less prone to death when you reveal and live in your purpose.

When your true purpose makes an appearance, these changes become exponentially stronger. I'm not prone to make assumptions, but... cough.... cough! There is a proverb from King Solomon that says where there is no vision, the people perish. Where purpose is not present, vision also does not make an appearance. These studies support this wise proverb.

Living Healthier

The health benefits that accompany the presence of your life's purpose are plentiful. A few that I will highlight are well-being, less disease, and better sleep. Several studies out there support all of these benefits. For the sake of brevity, I will highlight a few that relate to these benefits.

Well-Being

Many studies surround the realm of purpose in life and point to its association with well-being. In the world of psychology, sociology, and any of the other disciplines, well-being has been a popular topic. To my surprise, hundreds of studies and articles in academic journals offer great depth to the relationship between purpose, meaning in life, and well-being.

The only thing is well-being could be understood to mean many different things. There isn't one definition of well-being that is set in stone. Although, as a whole, well-being is a general sense of *wellness* in areas including but not limited to physical, mental, social, and psychological function, cognition, and life satisfaction.

In one particular study, which I will reference a few times, the authors sought to find the correlations in the relationship between the presence and the search for meaning in life with four factors: age, physical well-being, mental well-being, and cognitive functioning. In case you sped past that last sentence, take note of the difference between the *presence of* meaning in life and the *search for* meaning in life.

Physical well-being is the overall health of your body. Mental well-being is the overall health of your psychological state. Cognitive functioning includes mental abilities such as memory, learning, thinking, reasoning, problem-solving, and decision-making. The study is titled "*Meaning in Life and its Relationship with Physical, Mental, and Cognitive Functioning: A Study of 1,042 Community-Dwelling Adults across the Lifespan.*"

The study examined 1,042 adults in San Diego, CA, between the ages of 21 and 100+. With physical well-being and mental well-being, the findings were as follows. The presence of meaning in life proved to increase overall physical and mental well-being across all ages. The presence of meaning also showed increased cognitive function in older adults. The search for meaning in life decreased overall physical and mental well-being across all ages. The search for meaning also showed decreased cognitive function in older adults. The authors also state that purpose in life is significantly associated with cognitive function across all age groups.

In another study titled "Purpose in Life and Cognitive Functioning in Adulthood" 9, the authors tested middle to older-aged adults to discover the link between purpose in life and cognitive functioning. The study included nearly 3500 people between the ages of 32 and 84. This study also found that higher levels of purpose are related to higher cognitive functioning.

What does all that mean? It means that when people don't feel a sense of meaning in life, their physical and mental health declines. But your physical and mental health increases when meaning and purpose are felt and present. It's almost as if purpose and meaning protect the universal resources everyone has.

Again, take note of how the search for meaning in life and the presence of meaning in life have opposing effects on us. Purpose *and* meaning in life increase overall well-being, but when they aren't present, overall well-being decreases. This shows the importance of finding purpose in life as soon as possible. Its presence isn't just to make you healthier; it also prevents the decay that occurs when it is missing.

Less Disease

People who live *without* a sense of purpose are 2.7x more likely to die from heart disease, 2.1x more likely to die from digestive disease, and 1.2x more likely to die from cancer. The same study mentioned earlier titled, "Association between life purpose and mortality among us adults older than 50 years" 3, revealed this data after studying nearly 7,000 individuals over 50 to see if there is a correlation between life purpose and mortality. Living with purpose adds years to your life and gives you more *life* while you're here on this Earth.

I'd like to draw special attention to the most significant finding from this study. Individuals are 2.7x more likely to die from heart disease than people living their life *on* purpose. Why do I want you to pay special attention to this statistic? Take a wild guess at what the #1 cause of death is in the United States of America.

If you guessed heart disease, then you guessed right. At the time of this writing, heart disease has been the leading cause of death in the US for *at least* 6 years. The only other cause of death that is even close is cancer. Except for cancer, heart disease kills nearly 6x times more people than any other cause of death in the US...every year2.

Table. Number of Deaths for Leading Causes of Death, US, 2015-2020[a]

Cause of death	No. of deaths by year					
	2015	2016	2017	2018	2019	2020
Total deaths	2 712 630	2 744 248	2 813 503	2 839 205	2 854 838	3 158 814
Heart disease	633 842	635 260	647 457	655 381	659 041	690 882
Cancer	595 930	598 038	599 108	599 274	599 601	598 932
COVID-19[b]						345 323
Unintentional injuries	146 571	161 374	169 936	167 127	173 040	192 176
Stroke	140 323	142 142	146 383	147 810	150 005	159 050
Chronic lower respiratory diseases	155 041	154 596	160 201	159 486	156 979	151 637
Alzheimer disease	110 561	116 103	121 404	122 019	121 499	133 382
Diabetes	79 535	80 058	83 564	84 946	87 647	101 106
Influenza and pneumonia	57 062	51 537	55 672	59 120	49 783	53 495
Kidney disease	49 959	50 046	50 633	51 386	51 565	52 260
Suicide	44 193	44 965	47 173	48 344	47 511	44 834

[a] Leading causes are classified according to underlying cause and presented according to the number of deaths among US residents. For more information, see the article by Heron.[4] Source: National Center for Health Statistics. National Vital Statistics System mortality statistics (http://www.cdc.gov/nchs/deaths.htm). Data for 2015-2019 are final; data for 2020 are provisional.

[b] Deaths with confirmed or presumed COVID-19, coded to International Statistical Classification of Diseases and Related Health Problems, Tenth Revision code U071 as the underlying cause of death.

Let me remind you of all the factors that *don't* impact this statistic. Even after taking into account other variables like exercise, age (50-80), sex, education level, anxiety, depression, race, marital status, smoking status, functional status, frequency of physical activity, alcoholic consumption, presence of chronic health conditions, body mass index, depression, anxiety, clinical hostility, optimism, and social participation the mortality rate was still 2.7x higher with people who had little or no sense of purpose!!

In essence, _none_ of these factors impact the study's results. It doesn't matter if you are black, white, or purple. You could have a Ph.D. or be lacking a high school diploma. That pack of cigarettes you smoke every day doesn't change this baseline for you. A person with a chronic health condition and another person as healthy as an ox is still affected the same. Are you an optimistic person or a pessimistic person? The results revealed that none of these individual factors have a say. Here is the bottom line. If you live your life outside of purpose, you are 2.7x more likely to die from heart disease, 2.1x more likely to die from digestive disease, and 1.2x more likely to die from cancer.

What does this mean for you? It means your life's purpose may be more important than you've given it credit for. You should give it more attention than you have been. It deserves more time from you. The mere fact that the number one cause of death in the US and the highest multiplier of death found from a lack of purpose in life are the same should be alarming.

This sheds light on the importance of knowing and living in your purpose. If you picked up this book, it says a lot about who you are. It speaks volumes about who you will become in due time. You are headed in the right direction. Don't give up along the way. Your life depends on it...literally.

Better Sleep

Because we spend nearly 1/3 of our lives asleep, it is vital to ensure that we make the most of that time. Statistics show that 32–45% of older adults report having difficulty falling asleep, staying asleep, or having undisrupted sleep14. Nearly 40% of older adults suffer from a sleep disorder14. In addition, studies have also revealed that sleep difficulties are linked to depression, heart disease, and impaired physical functioning14.

One particular study, "Is *purpose in life associated with less sleep disturbance in older adults?*" 14, aimed to seek further findings in the relationship between purpose in life and sleep quality. The authors sought to reveal the relationship between purpose in life and three specific sleep disorders in older adults: sleep apnea, restless leg syndrome, and REM behavior disorder. Over 800 people were assessed in this study. Researchers performed annual follow-ups with participants over three years to determine any changes in sleep patterns.

Their findings supported their hypothesis of higher levels of purpose being associated with better sleep quality. The authors also stated that purpose in life appears to have protective characteristics against sleep disorders and symptoms of sleep apnea and restless leg syndrome.

This is one of a handful of studies focusing on sleep quality and purpose in life. That third of your life you spend at rest can improve when you start living on purpose. You would think that your purpose in life would have little impact on your sleep quality. However, the benefits of living purposefully are much more comprehensive than the mind can fathom.

As I previously stated, these three items are merely the tip of the iceberg regarding the many benefits of purpose on our health. The bottom line lies in the awareness these studies bring. The awareness reveals the fact that all of these benefits await you. They lie dormant, waiting to be activated by the revelation and embodiment of *your* unique, purposeful life.

Living Wealthier Through Business

It is shockingly evident what purpose in life can do for you. But, there is another area where studies show that purpose plays a significant role...business! While the purpose of business may not be the same as the purpose of your life. Suppose you bring your purpose in life into the realm of business. In that case, you may reap the benefits I listed above, alongside some revealing findings about purpose and its association with business.

If you take your life's purpose and align it with the mission and core of your business, you'll be met with the following advantages. More than 80% of Americans report having a positive image of, trust in, and loyalty to brands that lead with purpose10. Brands that lead with their purpose have grown 175% over the last 15 years, in contrast with a growth rate of 70% of companies that don't8.

From 1996-2013, purpose-driven companies grew by nearly 1681%. In that same timeframe, America's top 500 companies grew by an average of 118%. Purpose-driven companies grew 14 times faster than those in the S&P 500. That means you can add a 16.8x multiplier to your bottom line just for leading with purpose in your business11.

Even when recruiting new employees, having purpose as the core of your business is a genius business move. 80% of college graduates state it's very important or essential to get a strong sense of purpose from their choice of employment. However, only 50% of college graduates can find any remanence of purpose in their work4. This means a sizeable gap exists in the market for companies to hire more qualified and eager personnel when they lead with purpose. In addition, the best employees, the Crim de la crème, are 3x more likely to work with a business that displays and operates from a strong sense of purpose5.

The number of people interested in escaping the corporate world, also called "The Rat Race," steadily increases with time. The statistics continue to show that having purpose as your business's core message and foundation is one of the most helpful practices.

When you also consider the number of businesses that fail in the beginning stages, it is vital to use purpose in your business as a *boost* out of the land of failure. Again, this is one of the many realms of life where purpose makes things stronger, better, and faster. Purpose holds the transformative touch of Midas. Everything that it touches seems to turn to gold!

Coach's Challenge: Do you see the significance of knowing and living in your purpose!? It unlocks so many benefits that enhance your life. Here's a challenge that can enhance your awareness of just how vital your purpose is. Take the time to write out how having a longer life, less disease, better sleep, increased well-being, and more wealth could better your life.

Pro Tip: If you're not much of a writer, take out your phone and record yourself talking about how the above five topics would change your life if they all were enhanced. Whether you choose to write or speak, let your heart pour out. Refrain from being worried about being correct. Only concern yourself with being authentic.

Timing of Purpose

Limitation and uncertainty are two characteristics of time that no one can escape. Everybody's time is limited. One day, it will run out. Whatever that day and time is, its certainty is uncertain to every living soul. Nobody can escape these truths, no matter how you look at them. That's why there is so much significance in taking advantage of your time.

A particular *timing* of purpose is attached to it. The study I used earlier to reference well-being presented two other interesting findings3. As a reminder, the study examined the presence of and the search for meaning in life. First, the age gap where the *search for* meaning was most prevalent was between ages 20 and 30. Second, the age where the *presence of* meaning was most prevalent was age 60. Combining these two findings reveals a significant third finding. The gap between the onset of the search and the presence of meaning is 30-40 years.

That's anywhere between 10,950 and 14,600 days. Accepting those odds with a resource of an unknown and limited quantity is a gamble you shouldn't be willing to take. Everyone may not be blessed with that much time. Also, if you are blessed with that time, who wants to wait *that* long before their life is overflowing with meaning? Time is of the essence.

I've mentioned that meaning and purpose are different. However, I've referenced a study that primarily talks about meaning in life and secondarily addresses purpose in life. I included it for a specific reason. It is important to note that purpose drives meaning. That implies that meaning appears within a fashionable timeframe when purpose is present. When you reveal your purpose, you can finally live a life full of significance. Meaning will take on a whole new *meaning* in your life.

While purpose and meaning may be different, they are related to one another. Where one is, there the other will be as well. But one thing the researcher could never know is whether the meaning felt at age 60 was a result of *true purpose*. Was it because their eternal purpose or their external desires were realized? Scientific research does and will always have its limitations. If this is what the statistics show for meaning in life, what could it mean for *true* purpose?

I wanted to bring light to this because it is apparent that people within our world are not seeking their dharma...their ikigai. This could be due to a large number of reasons. The seemingly impossible nature of the task. The lack of interest in the topic across all cultures. The exceeding interest in the things of this world. The lack of people who can say that they have revealed and are living in their purpose. Any combination or one of all of these things could be a contributor.

The bottom line is it can take significantly less than 30-40 years. It doesn't have to take 3-4 years. With the right tools and environment, you can shave nearly all that time off. Remember that time is uncertain and limited. Be sure to reveal your purpose in life before your time is up. Commit to beating this statistic (by a long shot) so you can take advantage of the others that I mentioned.

Chapter 2 Summary:

- Your purpose is a magic pill. A pill that promises improvements in longevity, memory, sleep, decision-making, problem-solving, reasoning, overall health, financial well-being, and emotional states. Side effects include joy, peace, and resilience. The pills are accessible to anyone in unlimited quantities for free. Living in alignment with your purpose is the equivalent of taking this magic pill.

- Several studies provide clear evidence that individuals with a clear sense of purpose live longer than those who do not have a clear sense of purpose. To be specific, the mortality rate is 2.4x higher for those who lack awareness of their purpose. This shocking truth still holds weight in the face of factors like age, race, and depression.

- Purpose plays a pivotal role in well-being, disease prevention, and sleep habits. Individuals without a sense of purpose are more likely to die from heart disease (2.7x), digestive disease, and cancer. Purpose also acts protectively against sleep disorders like sleep apnea, restless leg syndrome, and REM behavior disorder.

- Purpose-driven businesses outperform their counterparts in various aspects. Purpose is a catalyst for success, influencing consumer perception, financial growth, and the attraction of top-tier talent. Infusing purpose into your professional endeavors can lead to a wealthier and more fulfilling business journey.

- Time is a finite and unpredictable resource, and we all should capitalize on the time at hand to unveil purpose. You don't have to wait for decades to discover your purpose. The process can be expedited with the right tools and environment, and you can enjoy the countless benefits of a purpose-driven life.

CHAPTER 3

THE PATHWAYS:

The 3 Pathways That Lead To Your Divine Purpose

"Don't go where the path may lead. Go where there is no path and leave a trail."

— **Les Brown**

I thought I was drowning as I looked up at my older brother with a grin on his face and an empty pot in his hand. One night, when we were teenagers, one of our cousins stayed at our house, and we played practical jokes all night. My big brother started the madness as he exclaimed, "The first one to fall asleep is gonna get it!" Since he put the word of caution into the atmosphere, we all knew to stay up as long as we could if we didn't want to be the butt of any jokes.

My cousin was the first to fall asleep. We put mustard on his hand and tickled his nose as we watched him slap a handful on his face. My brother was next. I woke up my cousin, and we did the same thing to him but with hot sauce. Out of paranoia, I was the last one to fall asleep. I waited until everyone else was fast asleep before I dozed off. But the other two must've been waiting for me.

In the middle of my sleep, I was awakened by my brother grinning over me with an empty pot. He tossed a pot of water on my face while I was inside my bed. He and my cousin laughed hysterically at my reaction as I gasped for air in confusion. That was the most severe abruption I'd ever experienced in my life. Getting cold water thrown on your face while awake would be startling. Having it done while you are asleep only magnifies the shock.

The older I get, the more I notice people living in a slumber. Every day, I see multiple people reliving the same nightmare. Even worse, they don't realize why they feel like they do. Over and over, they ignore entirely the precious resources and gifts that make them unique. It's almost as if people choose to go around the same circle and look away from the exit labeled as the pathway to purpose. Then, one day, life throws a pot of empty water on their face. Immediately, they realize that they've been asleep for dozens of years.

They've spent most of their energy *killing time with nothing to look forward to.* I am sure you are familiar with the phrase, "I am just trying to kill five minutes before..." I find it odd that we would refer to a resource as having a life that we desire to *kill.* Nevertheless, as this proverbial pot of water wakes you from your spiritual coma, your awareness is given life. The awareness often opens your mind to life's biggest questions. Why am I here? Where am I going? Who am I? Where did I come from? What can I do? These questions reveal the path of purpose.

I call this moment *the trigger*. A trigger is an external event that awakens your true Self. We've all had triggers in our life. They are needed. Without them, we'd never wake up. We would continue to live life never having lived at all. To have lived an entire life without purpose is to not have lived at all. Your triggers are the very objects that open your mind to Truth. Think about an alarm clock. It only exists to wake you up before it is too late.

The energy a trigger creates is often wasted on something other than the pursuit of purpose. Depression, feelings of inadequacy, escapism, and others can rob us of the clarity that a trigger can create. The worries and cares of this world can act as a blindfold the moment our trigger wakes us up.

However, there is also a choice to harness the energy and use it to confidently seek out the answers to the questions of life along the path of purpose. The path has always been there. The trigger is what opens up the mind to its presence.

As you walk up the path of purpose, it begins to split into three pathways: 1) Reactive, 2) Proactive, and 3) Interactive. All three pathways lead to your purpose. Often, the choice is unconscious. The natural tendency toward reward-seeking or pain avoidance moves you towards one pathway versus another.

One way isn't superior to another. It is not a matter of right versus wrong. It is simply a matter of choosing a path and creating movement. Sticking to one path is not the priority. The priority is getting to the result.

The Reactive Pathway

Pain Avoidance

If you are motivated by the avoidance of pain, you would be more prone to take the reactive route towards the revelation of your purpose in life. Some people are naturally more motivated by the avoidance of pain versus the gain of a reward. There is nothing wrong with this; it is just a different preference. They prefer to settle into a routine of predictability. If this sounds like a description of you, then the reactive pathway is one you may subconsciously lean towards.

Fear of the unknown inevitably leads to the shrinking of the Self. Read that last line again. Stepping out on faith is a challenging task to accomplish. When fear is present in your life, it can be challenging to take an active approach in the pursuit of purpose. That's a tricky question to go searching for an answer to. Not only that but if you found the answer, what would that mean for your current life? Would you be willing to leave the life you've spent so much time and energy building? What if what you have spent the last 10, 20, 30, or even 40 years pursuing is *misaligned with* your life's purpose?

These questions will be present even if they don't consciously populate your mind. These questions will be present in your subconscious. Fear, doubt, and worry will speak within your conscience comments that shut down the idea of revealing your purpose. On a lighter note, a reactive stance does hold the positive trait of having enough stored energy to react to the very trigger that life may give you as a "wake-up call."

The Trigger of Abruption

The trigger on the reactive pathway is often loud, aggressive, and disruptive. It has to be to do its job. The trigger is the very stimulus that wakes you up from the day-to-day routine of life that has you in a trance. You see, we all have routines in life.

Ninety-five percent of the population lives in what many people like to refer to as "The Rat Race." Monday through Friday becomes a form of Groundhog Day. Instead of it being a day, the same *week* is repeated over again. *Especially* once you enter adulthood. Usually, we don't seek answers to life's biggest questions until we experience a "trigger" powerful enough to disrupt the trance the world has placed upon us.

Like a runner waiting anxiously for the trigger of the starter pistol to sound so they can begin their race, our true Self awaits *every day* for some transformative event to take the place of that starter pistol and sound off so our true Self can begin his or her journey.

Unfortunately, the "trigger" that holds enough power to *wake us up* from our slumber at the starting line is usually one of life's greater tragedies. The trigger is usually accompanied by death, near-death experiences, significant loss, health problems, or some other extreme change that is unwanted in our lives. For those more proactive about their journey, the trigger can be as small as a conversation. It just depends on how deep you slumber. The deeper you are in the trance of your groundhog week, the bigger the trigger needs to be for you to wake up.

There comes a moment when you can see the end of your path. This is when most ask themselves, "Is this all there is?" How you respond to this question determines your life. This is when you start to pursue a life of purpose and meaning. Or this is when you look at the hand of life you have been dealt and accept what has become in your life.

For me, it was a conversation I had with my Pop when I was around 18. I'll never forget it. We were in his black 1999 Ford Expedition. My Pop was driving. My aunt was fast asleep, per usual, in the front seat. My older cousin, Vance, sat beside me in the back seat, blasting his headphones, and I was sitting behind Pop...asking questions about life!

I was telling him how lucky I thought I was that I'd gotten to live with him and my aunt (My Pop is really my uncle, but over the years, as the relationship grew, he became Pop, and I became Nephson). After I got through telling him that I thought I'd be in a horrible spot in life if I hadn't been so lucky, he turned and told me there's no such thing as luck. I can still feel the goosebumps just imagining the conversation.

He turned around with such seriousness and authority. The transition in his tone took me by surprise. He proceeded to tell me that God has a plan for everything. He continued, "Nothing happens outside of His plan, and you are exactly where you are for a reason." I sat there in silence. All I could muster up the courage to say was, "I'm here for a reason?"

He didn't turn around this time but continued to tell me, "There is a reason for everything...including you"! Immediately, my eyes started to well up with tears. I fought with everything in me to hold back the tears. I couldn't stop thinking to myself, "I have a purpose? I am here for a reason? Why am I here?"

That wasn't the first time I asked myself these questions. But it was the first time I had thought about them in years. I knew I had to be here on this Earth for a reason! I didn't say a word for the rest of the car ride. I couldn't get the image of that bullet hole through the headrest of the driver seat in my car out of my head. That conversation reminded me that I probably should have been dead.

I got my first car just a little after I turned 16. A few months later, one of my cousins was throwing a party (that later ended up on the news) at his home. His mom was out of town. It created an opportune time to have a night of fun. I called my father to ask if I could go to the party. His first response was, "Is his mom going to be there?" in his deep baritone voice. After I told him no, he told me I was not allowed to attend the party as any sane parent would. But I had already told one of my other cousins he could ride with me to the party. So, I went anyways...

As we arrived, there were at least 50 people outside. We could hear the music coming from inside the house as soon as we hit the corner. Some people were shooting dice in the garage. A few were lounging on the cars with drinks in their hand. Others were just standing around talking. I decided to park in the driveway since I knew the guy hosting the party. As we jumped out of the car, I was greeted by a few guys I played with on the basketball team.

I proceeded through the garage where the dice game was being played and gave a few more greetings to familiar faces along the way. As we stepped into the house, the first thing I noticed was how many people were inside. There were at least 100 people jam-packed into this small 3-bedroom, 2-bath house.

Bumping through the crowd, I walked around the house to greet as many people as possible. At that age, it was all about being seen. After making my rounds, my cousin and I decided to sit on the washer and dryer in the dining room since there was no other space to relax in the chaos.

After a few moments, I heard gunshots. As I sat on the dryer, I watched everyone have an obscene amount of panic. This was a regular occurrence at house parties, so I didn't think much of it. I continued to sit there for a few seconds. I looked over to my right, and the first thing I noticed was that my cousin had fled the house with everyone else.

As I jumped down from the dryer, the house was completely empty within the few seconds that had passed. I walked through an empty living room and out the front door. I look to my left from the front porch, and the first person I see is my cousin, who rode with me to the party. He started yelling with terror as he crossed the threshold between the garage and the driveway where my car was.

As I looked towards where his gaze was, the first thing I noticed was a pool of blood. The second thing I noticed was the body that was lying in it. As my cousin and I moved closer, I noticed his face was dripping with tears. He later told me he had thought the body belonged to his older brother, who had thrown the party. The young boy's body was lying directly next to the driver's door of my car.

I then shifted my gaze from the body to my baby blue 1990 Cadillac Seville. I then realized that my car had received quite a few bullets from the shootout. I started to scream at the top of my lungs out of confusion, anger, and shock from the situation. We both started to hear police sirens. We knew we couldn't be next to a dead body after a shootout as the police arrived. So we left...

But the problem was that the body was so close to my car that I had to step over it to get into my car. In addition, as I opened the driver's door, I noticed that there was a bullet going through the headrest in the driver's seat. The thought that I would've died had I been in my car just a few moments earlier appeared in my mind. Looking down at the body as I stepped over him, I couldn't help but feel like that could've just as easily been me. I immediately felt a rush of tears coming down my face.

My cousin got into the car, and we quickly proceeded out of the driveway to be gone by the time the police arrived. Just as I was exiting the driveway, I looked up, and another guy was holding the body that I had just stepped over to get in my car and leave. My headlights illuminated the two of them, and I could hear the guy screaming for help. But my fear propelled me to leave despite my spirit's urge to stop and help.

Driving down the street, I couldn't stop crying as I was full of so many different emotions. I began punching the steering wheel in frustration and screaming at the top of my lungs. I looked at my cousin in the passenger seat and saw the tears pouring down his face. Looking back down the lonely road, we began passing the cop cars on their way to the scene we had just left.

That was one of the longest nights of my life. For days, I couldn't stop thinking about that bullet through the headrest of the driver's seat and the dead body. I felt as though that could've easily been me. I'd be dead if I had decided to get in the driver's seat just minutes earlier and leave.

That incident is what made those words from my Pop trigger a "wake-up call" in my mind. Those few words, "There is a reason for everything...including you", were like water being thrown on my face in the middle of a good night's sleep.

Have you ever met somebody who continued to have "bad" things happen to them? I am convinced that if you ignore "triggers," they will continue to sound off until you heed the call. When I say ignoring a trigger, I mean allowing the energy created from a trigger to be used for something other than allowing your true Self to begin or continue along with its race.

One trigger sounds off...BANG! You stay at the starting line, sound asleep. Then another goes off, "BANG"! You roll over to the other side. Then another goes off, "BANG"! Are you willing to start the race? This doesn't imply that nothing terrible will ever happen after you've heard and received your "trigger." Many are the afflictions of the righteous. But trials of many kinds are not a punishment of some sort. Trials are merely the coach of life screaming at you along the sideline of your race. Telling you to keep going, pick up your knees, focus, and finish your race.

The Proactive Pathway

Reward Seeking

The proactive road to purpose is a wise road to take. Natural tendencies will show that people who take the proactive path are naturally curious. Being highly motivated by seeking rewards, there is no block to putting oneself into situations involving uncertainty. I admire those who prefer the path of proactivity because of the courage in their steps.

Something about the curiosity of the unknown inevitably leads to the expansion of Self. The fear of the unknown cannot independently create this *expansion of Self*. This is a characteristic of many people deemed by society to be "successful." The proactive path is full of courage.

According to Dr. David Hawkins' book Power vs. Force, courage is the point along the scale of consciousness that forces a transition into power. Courage and fear hold vast differences in their approach to execution. Anywhere fear is present, the presence of force will also be there. Think of someone who tries to "force" a relationship.

Consider the damage that can be done to a pegboard by forcing a square peg into a round hole. Someone can exert so much force that they slip a disc in their back. Or, someone could be *forced* to do something against their will. Force often leaves its subject damaged after it does its work. It's almost as if our "trigger" is trying to "force" us into having the courage to start the race.

In contrast, the presence of power will be anywhere courage is. Where force leaves the residue of damage, power leaves the residue of advancement. Think about an engine's power, electricity, water, fire, light, belief, etc. Have you ever referred to any of these things as a force? We never associate objects of true power with force. Therefore, the power associated with proactivity should be sought after.

Does this imply that reactivity is weak? Of course, reactivity is not weak. However, a massive drawback to reactivity is its inherent dangers. Force is literally a "force of nature." Its elements impose their will upon its subject. Force is power uncontrolled. Think about strong forces of nature such as a tornado, tsunami, earthquake, or volcanic eruption. They hold large amounts of power but tend to damage or destroy when imposed.

The Gradual Trigger

The trigger of the proactive road is much more subtle than the reactive road's. Clarification is usually reached at a much slower pace on this road. It will take time and patience. These are the characteristics that come along with taking this route. Whereas the trigger that comes along the reactive road must be loud and disruptive, the trigger on the proactive road can do its job without having to cause a disruption.

Awareness is the difference. An Olympic runner who has trained and done all they can to be ready for the moment the starter pistol fires will be anticipating the trigger. Ready to reap the harvest of all their sowing into purpose.

The proactive road is a slow marathon. The fact that these individuals are usually motivated by rewards is a plus. Because they know a reward awaits them at the end, they have a higher endurance within them. They can keep a steady pace with their eyes focused on the reward. This adds resilience to their lives. It could be linked to the empirical data that reveals increases in resilience alongside the presence of purpose.

If you're reading this, you may have been seeking out your purpose and drawn into this material. If so, congrats to you. After all, what good is it to have gained the world just to lose your soul? Living a good life without living the *right* life would be a tragedy!

The Interactive Pathway

The third road is the interactive road. The collaborative use of proactivity and reactivity along your journey towards purpose. This combines the power of proactivity and the energy of reactivity. Naturally, things in life will occur. Unfortunately, great tragedy can often be the trigger that opens our minds to the path of purpose.

To the malleable mind, a crisis can be the *wake-up call* that our soul needs. As discussed earlier, life's greatest transformative moments occur on the reactive path. However, being proactive puts you on the journey earlier, increasing your chances of revealing your true purpose and putting you in a ready stance for whatever comes your way. When tragedy strikes, you're more able to transmute the energy from the tragedy into energy that the Self can use to grow.

Similar to the process that a caterpillar uses to evolve. A caterpillar breaks down its body and uses it as energy to develop its evolved butterfly form. Using that energy to your benefit can provide what you need to evolve. Now, this doesn't imply that one should look forward to the great tragedies of life.

However, with a proactive perspective, you can be put in a position to overcome the tragedy better and stronger than before. It's quite a better position to be in versus the man or woman who is struck by surprise so powerfully that you lose all consciousness of life and go into a deep sleep mentally that removes you from the world as you know it.

Following Your Passions

Along the path that leads you to reveal and embody your purpose in life, your passions will play an integral role. Within the pathways to purpose framework, it is necessary to distinguish between pleasure and passion.

Our culture tells us in various ways that the adage "follow your passion" is the way of purpose. While passions certainly have a part in the realm of purpose in life, it is not safe to conclude that passions are your purpose in life. First, many people confuse passions with pleasures. Second, many such "passions" bring more chaos and confusion than order and clarity.

In differentiating passion and pleasure, there are specific characteristics the two hold that oppose one another. As human beings, we all have needs that disturb homeostasis when they aren't met. Needs include shelter, food, water, safety, reproduction, etc. The disruption of homeostasis is only satisfied once the needs are met.

Many of the mediums used to satisfy these needs are highly comforting. Not only are they comforting, but we've also enhanced these mediums in innovative ways over centuries. These new innovative ways satisfy our needs, but they allow us to do so faster, better, and, in some cases, in unlimited variety. Because of this, it is easy to overindulge and perform activities that violate the natural laws of our world.

I won't name them all, but just think of the many ways we have created to satisfy the needs of reproduction, safety, drink, and food. Most of these innovations do more harm than good. This is just the tip of the iceberg. Many of these activities are deemed to be pleasurable. Things of pleasure usually satisfy the basic needs but can do so in pervasive and excessive ways.

The Key of Sharing

So, what is the difference between a pleasure and a passion? Three distinct keys will open the door to understanding the difference between pleasures and passions. The first key is the key of sharing. Mostly, every pleasure can only be openly shared if the people it is shared with hold similar beliefs about it. Pleasures are usually kept secret. Not always, though. Some pleasures, such as the excessive use of alcohol, have become so widely accepted that some of us will allow our children to drink.

Another aspect of this key is the sharing of the enjoyment. When something is done for pleasure, it is nearly always done for selfish reasons. Even though others may be participating in the act with you, you're merely doing it for yourself. Being able to do it with others just enhances the experience.

Passions, on the other hand, are nearly always able to be enjoyed by large masses of diverse crowds with different beliefs. In some cases, sports, art, or even science are great examples. This may go without being said, but note that this small list isn't exclusive. These can all be enjoyed in public without remorse or shame.

In addition, these aren't merely done for self-enjoyment but for sharing energy and enjoyment with others. If pleasure is a taker, then passion is a giver. Your passions will give you energy. Pleasure will take your energy. This is also one of the reasons why people will gather to see someone in their passion. To receive energy and life. When done with significant skill levels, the giving can be done with large masses of people.

The Key of Control

The second key is the key of control. Many pleasures can control you. They have somewhat of an ability to put their users in a sort of trance. Pleasure can be very addictive. This is not to be confused with the state of flow.

The flow state is similar to this trance when specific characteristics are met. With flow, when the activity ends, the flow state ends with it. With many pleasures, it is the exact opposite. The trance consumes you. It floods your mind with images and distracts you from day-to-day activities. With passions, this is not so. With passions, we maintain control. As a matter of fact, many people who experience a state of flow with their passions state that they experience heightened levels of control.

The basketball player in a flow state has complete control and awareness of everything happening. The dancer would explain their state of flow as everything happening in slow motion and being keen and deliberate about every movement made. This is another reason why others enjoy observing passions. Witnessing flow in action is a remarkable experience.

The flow of passion doesn't control and consume like the trance of pleasure. Day-to-day activities can be resumed. The constant thinking of a passion only enhances life, where pleasures that flood the mind obstruct life with a neverending demand for fulfillment that can never be obtained. This is because pleasures can not be fulfilled but only suppressed. Suppressions come with escapism, slavery, and strife. Passions, conversely, can be fulfilled, and with fulfillment comes joy, peace, and freedom.

The Key of Use

Lastly is the key of use. Pleasures are almost always associated with immoral activities. These forms of enjoyment come with a price to pay. When you sow a bad seed, you cannot reap the harvest of a good tree. When immoral activities are engaged, you are sowing bad seeds.

This may come with a moment of relief, but when harvest time approaches, you will only find discord. This is why the overuse of moral pleasures and the use of immoral pleasures will hinder your life in one or more ways. In contrast, the extended use of passions will lead to advancement in one or more areas of life. The use of passions will challenge you, and pleasures will stagnate you. Using a passion will result in a new or improved skill, while using pleasure will leave you drained.

Please don't misunderstand this to mean that passions are not meant to be enjoyable. Passions will have sustained moments of joy and satisfaction. Similar to the previous mention of Power vs. Force, the difference lies in control. Passion and pleasure are both enjoyable. However, pleasure takes satisfaction of the senses and gives it a multiplier.

When the power of passion is released, it will control the presence of good feelings. In a way, your passions can be like a governor for sensual satisfaction. The same energy that can consume you in pleasure is directed healthily by passion. Indulgence by itself is like allowing a toddler to have his own home. But with passion, it's like giving that toddler a parent to watch over him. If pleasure is selfish, then passion is giving. If pleasure is immoral, then passions are upright. If pleasure is out of control, passions are disciplined.

This concept holds substantial significance around the topic of purpose in life. The message spoken for decades has been, "Follow your passion!" While this statement holds some validity, it is also dangerous for two reasons: 1) Most people don't know the difference between their pleasures and their passions, and 2) Your passions are not your purpose in life.

Many times, pleasure can masquerade as passion. This is why it is so easy to confuse pleasure with passion. They both come with strong feelings. Not understanding the difference between the two can leave you enslaved to your pleasures. In contrast, you become the director of your passions when you can clearly distinguish the two.

If you can't tell the difference between pleasure and passion, you can end up in a revolving door of mediocrity. Pleasure and passion are like fraternal twins. They can look practically identical but have different genetic makeup. Passions will always move you toward more elevated giving, freeing, and advancement levels. Conversely, pleasure will always keep you in a revolving door of selfishness, disorder, and stagnation.

When, and only when, what you see as your passions meet these characteristics should you allow them to direct you along your journey. Simply, our passions are directional signs along the pathway of purpose. They tell you you are going the wrong way or the right way. Your passions will advise you that a left or right turn is approaching. While they may <u>not</u> be your life purpose, they are an essential part of the journey.

> **Coach's Challenge:** If you've already started your journey towards purpose, which pathways do you relate to the most? If you still need to start your journey, which pathways would you like to utilize? Here's another challenge. Spend 5-10 minutes journling about your pursuit of purpose. For those who have yet to begin their journey, how can you incorporate the pathway of purpose you'd like to utilize in the near future? For those who have already begun their journey, what triggers woke you from your slumber?

Chapter 3 Summary:

- Many people go throughout their lives in a slumber. Like the Israelites, most wander in circles, often missing out on their unique gifts and purpose. A "trigger" is often needed to awaken someone from their slumber.

- A trigger is an external event that serves as a wake-up call, bringing awareness to those who may have been living without purpose. Those on the Reactive Pathway experience an abrupt trigger that disrupts their routine and prompts them to question the meaning and purpose of their life. Those on the Proactive Pathway experience a more gradual trigger that won't disrupt life. In contrast, the Interactive Pathway combines both elements of the Reactive Pathway and the Proactive Pathway.

- It is often said that *following your passions* is how to find your purpose. You must understand the keys to differentiating passions from pleasures along your path to purpose. The three keys of passion are sharing, control, and use. Understanding these three can save you a lot of confusion along your journey.

- Everyone has a choice in responding to triggers. We must all actively seek purpose after being awakened by significant life events. Ignoring triggers might lead to a repetitive cycle until you acknowledge and respond to the wake-up calls.

CHAPTER 4

THE PERSPECTIVES:

The ONLY Way To Guarantee A Successful Life Experience

"You don't see things the way they are. You see things the way you are"

– Anais Nin

Choose Your Glasses Wisely

You might remember the DARE program when you were in school if you were near my age. For those who don't know, DARE is the name of an education program. The acronym stands for *Drug Abuse and Resistance Education* Program.

Their vision has been to teach the youth good decision-making skills to empower them to live free from violence and substance abuse regardless of their environment. The initiative has been around since 1983 and has grown into an international program! They travel to schools and give talks, have booths at events, hand out information packets, and even have live demonstrations.

One of their more popular demonstrations is a simulation of what it's like to have to walk a straight line while intoxicated. It involves putting a pair of *drunk goggles* on the kids and instructing them through a sobriety test. The goggles have distorted lenses that drastically impair your vision. Consequently, it reduces your sense of awareness and ability to react among other motor and cognitive functions.

When you put on the goggles, it becomes as if the world becomes a mirror maze. It is an attempt to show kids and teenagers the effects that alcohol has on your perception. Sometimes, they make you spin in circles before putting you through the challenge to make it more difficult. Some programs even have older students go through a driving course in a golf cart with drunk goggles on to see how drinking impairs their driving skills.

Our *perceptions* are like pairs of glasses we wear when walking through the domains of life. What is your perception like when you think of your purpose in life? Do you wear a pair of drunk goggles? Or have you chosen a pair of prescription glasses tailored to you?

I came up with the idea of the *perspectives of purpose* to show others what life looks like from the different "*glasses*" we can choose around the topic. It's meant to be like the demonstration that DARE officers use with drunk goggles.

The perspectives I'll show you will reveal how particular perspectives of life and purpose impair or boost your ability to function. We often use the word discover when thinking of purpose in life. You'll hear things like, "Have you discovered your purpose in life?" Or, "I'm still searching for my purpose in life" is often mentioned around the subject.

A Discovery implies that the subject at hand was once lost. I'd argue that your purpose has never been lost. You've just been looking through the wrong lens. You don't need to find your purpose. You just need to choose the correct perspective, and your purpose will be revealed.

The Pieces of The Perspectives

Three components form this model: 1) The three perspectives, 2) Your life's purpose, and 3) the Meaning within each perspective.

The Three Perspectives

The perspectives are the cornerstone of this model. There are three perspectives. From the bottom to the top are Obstruction, Obscurity, and Observation. So, *if* this model were to represent a state, there would be three cities. The cities of Obstruction, Obscurity, and Observation.

Each city has four precincts. The precincts can be likened to neighborhoods. You and I both know that every city has good and bad neighborhoods. Everyone operates differently. This is how the perspectives or purpose work.

Your Life's Purpose

Your purpose is the second component of the model. It serves as an essential theme for the model. Purpose stands true in all circumstances, but how individuals view purpose changes as their beliefs change (hence the different perspectives). Purpose does not change; only our perspective of purpose changes.

Just like God doesn't change, only our perception of him changes. God has a real image. His image depicts who he truly is and all the principles and values that make him who he is. Many people are in search of His true image. But as our perspective of who he is changes, does this imply that God also changes?

Well, of course not; only our perception of who he is changed. So then, the ultimate goal isn't to discover purpose but to reveal the proper perspective of purpose that has been there all along. Just like we don't need to discover or find God, we only need the correct perspective of who he is to have a radical change in our lives.

Focus

The third and final component is focus. With every perspective comes parallel levels of focus. *Within each perspective, the things that you focus on change.* As we go into what I like to call *the precincts* of each perspective, you will see more clearly how your focus in life changes in each perspective.

This is part of the reason many people perceive that their purpose changes. It isn't that their purpose has changed; their perspective of purpose has changed, and naturally, the things that matter to them have also changed. This is because the things you focus on typically have a grasp on your heart. The areas of life that you *pay* attention to matter to you the most.

This doesn't mean that what mattered to you previously no longer matters. Instead, it is to imply that matters of life that hold significance to us will be added and have varying levels of strength.

All About Perspective

Before we delve into the specifics, it would be beneficial to describe *perspective* in its general sense. A perspective is your view of the world. It is the way you see things. Now, a perspective can be an ally or an enemy.

More often than not, we don't see things as they are but how we believe them to be. Just because we believe something to be true doesn't make it the Truth. What is seen may not reveal all the details you need to fully interpret the situation. How, then, are perspectives created?

A perspective is based upon a belief. For example, let's say you were at a sports event inside of a dome. Most domes provide seating that allows you to sit anywhere within a full 360-degree radius of the action. Your belief would be synonymous with your seat placement inside the dome. A good belief would give you floor seats. You'd be able to see every detail of the game.

A poor belief would be like having nosebleed seats. You may be there, but your ability to see what's happening would be severely skewed. During the game, there is a controversial call by one of the referees. Your belief (your seat) would determine your perspective of the referees' call. Your belief will always place you in a specific position concerning the matter at hand.

In turn, your position will determine how you view the subject. The belief you have may put you in an empowering position. In contrast, your belief could put you at a disadvantage. This poses another question. How can you know when a belief will place you in an advantage versus a position with a disadvantage?

That answer is based upon the law. There are laws that govern everything. The laws will work for you if you have a *correct* belief, and you will work against the law if your belief puts you at a disadvantage. Yes, you will work *against* the law. This is like trying to move an immovable force.

Has there ever been a time when you felt that no matter what you did, you just couldn't make any progress? That's because you were working *against* a law. You were pushing against an immovable force. Keep in mind I am not talking about the laws of man, such as robbery or murder.

I am referencing the spiritual laws of the universe that God established during the genesis of Earth. The laws of Faith, polarity, cause & effect, advancement, attraction, detachment, vibration, and rhythm are some of the names we've given to a handful of these laws. Like the laws of gravity and lift, we cannot see them, but we feel their presence daily.

Thus, the beliefs *you choose about life's qualms* determine your perspective. Then, your perspective naturally determines whether you work with or against these laws. A compelling thought is that we *choose* the very vantage points that our perspectives place us.

The fact that we have a choice means that we also can willfully choose a different perspective should we choose to do so. So, then another question arises worthy of an answer. How is a perspective changed?

The easy answer is to change your beliefs. But as I'm sure you know, it's not always easy. As Isaac Newton so cleverly put it, an object at rest tends to stay at rest unless acted upon by an unbalanced force. This applies to many things in life, including your beliefs.

Sometimes, a huge life event is the catalyst that shakes up our belief system. Other times, it's as simple as the seed of a word taking root in your mind and overpowering your limiting beliefs. Someone else's words can be the shift that changes your perspective.

Having the right or wrong perspective comes down to whether you believe in the Truth or a lie. What happens to your perspective when you believe a lie? It's like intentionally placing a wall in front of your nosebleed seats at the sporting event I mentioned earlier. Even more so, believing a lie is like placing yourself in bondage.

Lies are a snare that locks you into a limited viewpoint. This is why Jesus said that *the Truth* will set you free. Free to do what? Free to move to a different vantage point that will allow you to see the Truth of a situation, person, place, or thing. But you have to believe the Truth before you see it, or else you will remain in bondage.

Concerning purpose, this model is all about helping others assess what their perspective may be. Understanding where your perspective lies along the spectrum of Truth can be challenging, but it's also essential. Suppose you can't recognize that you may have the wrong perspective about your purpose in life or anything else. In that case, you'll never be able to see the Truth.

Consequently, you'll never be free from the invisible forces that keep you locked into a limited viewpoint. In the game of life, you have the power to choose courtside seats, nosebleeds, or wander around the outside of the stadium.

The Perspectives

Now that we understand the model's purpose (no pun intended) and understand a perspective, we can discuss the three perspectives around purpose in life. Purpose will manifest in your lives in different ways within the three perspectives.

Hopefully, as you read this section, you will be met with a moment of Truth. A moment that opens your heart and allows the Truth to be planted. A moment of clarification and understanding of how purpose is manifesting in your life right now. Remember that you have the power to choose to shift perspectives at any time.

The Perspective of Obstruction

The first perspective is the perspective of Obstruction. The perspective of comfort. In this perspective, you have an obstructed view of your purpose in life. There is usually an inherent _comfortability_ and complacency in how you live.

A key sign of comfortability is a battle with change. Not only do you resist change, but you'll fight to keep your life as it is. You prefer the comfort of mediocrity over the challenge and eventual crowning of purpose.

Often, things appear to be fine on the outside, but the lack of growth in your life creates a void that comes with a constant sting. Knowing you have a sense of responsibility outside of your established routine increases the feeling that comes with the void that gnaws at your heart.

But the longer you ignore the call of purpose, the more it becomes background static. Similar to the sound of a refrigerator or central air. You may be hearing this or some other outside noise right now. It has fallen to the background without awareness. The words I just planted into your mind may have raised your awareness of the background noise.

This is how your life's purpose becomes when you believe the words of Obstruction. People with this perspective often say they don't believe they have a purpose for their life. Or that there is no meaning or purpose to life at all. Some even believe others have a purpose in life, but there's no way their life could have a purpose. These are all words of Obstruction.

The Perspective of Obscurity

The second perspective is one of Obscurity. From this perspective, life is a *challenge.* From one perspective, a challenge may seem "bad." But from the perspective of Obscurity, it is understood that a challenge is a gateway to a better life. The challenge is what creates a better and stronger you.

This is what the Apostle James means when he says to consider it pure joy to face trials of many kinds because the testing of Faith produces perseverance. Perseverance makes you mature and complete, not lacking anything. The difficulty of this perspective lies in the challenge. Not many people can persevere when it gets tough. Staying in a position of comfort is all too familiar and too easy.

Obscure means to be uncertain or unclear. Similar to looking through a frozen windshield that has yet to be fully defrosted. You have an idea of what's in front of you, but it's very unclear. Sometimes, you even have a small opening on the windshield that you can see out of. If you are in a rush, you may have had to drive looking through that small opening until the window defrosted. If you've ever been running behind for work in the morning, you may be able to relate. It's not a fun thing to do.

This perspective is similar to going through life looking through that tiny opening in your windshield. You can travel to far places in these conditions but it's not a comfortable feeling. From this perspective, you're not quite sure what your purpose is. You know you have a purpose in life. But you haven't given it much thought. The routine and worries in your mind have fogged up your life, and your view of your life's purpose is diminished.

The Perspective of Observation

The third perspective is the perspective of Observation. This is the perspective of _crowning_. When your purpose is observed, it provides clarity. This is the perspective of the Truth. Your purpose in life is known and understood. When you live in your purpose, you receive your crown. You can only claim the crown when you step up and take ownership of your province.

A little food for thought I'd like to add to this perspective. Many times, people associate their life purpose with a noteworthy victory. However, our life's purpose is often more aligned with sacrifice than the victory you may seek. Sometimes, the victory is found in some form of sacrifice.

The 4 Precincts of Perspective

So far, we've discussed three things: 1) What the 'Perspectives of Purpose' model is, 2) What a perspective is, and 3) What the three perspectives regarding purpose are. Next, we'll get into what I call the precincts of each purpose. What would it look like if all three perspectives I mentioned were three different cities? What values and beliefs would govern the people who live in each city?

Every city has different areas, or regions, within its makeup that we call neighborhoods. Typically, every neighborhood is entirely different than its surrounding areas. The people in one neighborhood may be focused on survival, while in another, the focus may be education. Every neighborhood functions differently.

Within the Perspectives of Purpose framework, these neighborhoods within each perspective are called precincts. A precinct is an area of town designated for specific or restricted use. For this model, a precinct will be seen as an area of life designated with a specific *focus*.

There are 4 different precincts. Each precinct manifests with a different focus when placed in a different perspective. A perspective's ability to direct your focus is where its true power lies. The way you view your purpose in life will shift your focus. The reason this is powerful is that focus breeds life. Why?

A quote says, "Where your focus goes, your energy flows." Where there is energy, there is life. This also means where there is no energy, there is no life. Each precinct will show you what your perspective about your purpose is causing you to focus on. Service, Span of Time, Sustenance, and Sight are the four precincts. All four are directly linked to your purpose in life. This is why when your perspective of purpose in life changes, so does your focus. I want to show you how each precinct shifts your focus differently in each perspective.

The Precinct of Service

Service is the bedrock of your purpose. When your perspective of purpose changes, so does your service. This is a direct correlation of how your focus within the realm of service will shift differently when your perspective changes. Your service is the act of helping or working. Three focuses exist within the precinct of service: Self, others, and humanity.

Finding where your focus is within this precinct is relatively simple. There are a few keys to remember as you go through this section.

First, the objective will be to find the *primary* focus. You need to find the focus that lies at the root of why you do the things you do, not what appears at the surface. There will be activities in your life that may mask themselves as one focus, but beneath the mask lies your true focus.

Second, as you read through this section, your ego will make an appearance. You have to recognize it when it arises and quiet the voice of your ego in your mind. If not, you won't be able to recognize how your perspective is guiding your focus in your life right now. You also won't realize how the proper perspective will manifest. Your ego will tell you that you're already there. Be cautious of its presence.

Self

From the perspective of Obstruction, service manifests itself with a primary focus on Self. The work that you do is for you. What you do in life is always centered around *you*. You only work if *you* are getting paid. Things only get done if *you* feel like doing the work. You only move if it benefits *you*. The only people you keep in your life are the ones who cater to *you*. If anything doesn't help *you*, have *you* at the center, or appeal to *you*, you want no part.

Two primary questions can reveal two things: 1) If your perspective of purpose is obstructed, and 2) If your focus has shifted your service toward selfishness.

First, would you still do it if there were no benefits for you? Do you only tap into your six resources when there is some benefit for yourself? Would you still deplete your time, energy, mind, and other resources if those benefits were removed?

Second, do I perform without complaining, blaming, or criticizing? Think about the areas of service in your life, such as parenthood, career, volunteer work, etc. Are you constantly complaining about something, blaming others, or criticizing? If you answered no to either of these questions, your perspective of purpose may be obstructed.

Others

When your perspective of purpose shifts to Obscurity, all areas of service in your life also shift focus. Your focus makes an important change to being centered around other people. You'll begin adding value to other people's lives. You tap into your six resources when the opportunity to be a blessing to someone else arises. Someone genuinely concerned for the well-being of another is someone who exhibits high levels of empathy.

There is a significant shift in focus from constantly looking at what you can receive to what you can give. You start creating things to help other people. When service manifests with a focus on other people, you will begin to see a significant change in your lives. This is because of the law of reciprocity. As you give, so shall you receive. Those who are always thinking of other people are givers.

When you transition from a taker to a giver, the law of reciprocity begins to work in your favor. When you are constantly planting seeds of growth, you will one day be harvesting crops of growth as long as you don't give up. So, the mere focus on other people begins to produce new growth in your life.

Humanity

When your true purpose appears, you've moved into the perspective of Observation. From this point of view, your perspective moves your focus of service to humanity. This focus is similar to focusing on others but on a grander scale.

This level of service is for those who genuinely connect with and live in their purpose at a high level. Having a clear, truthful perspective of your purpose manifests creativity that permeates all humans. Everyone, should they choose to, can benefit from the work that you offer to the world.

The solutions you create and the systems you build don't just impact you and those around you; they increase the experience of life for all of humanity. Not just humanity today but mankind of today, tomorrow, and forever. The only way to reach this caliber of focus is by tapping into a power source more powerful than yourself.

The Precinct of The Span of Time

Welcome to the second precinct, Span of Time. The main focus in this precinct concerns the length of time. What span of time are you focused on? Everyone has a relationship with time. More specifically, we feel most comfortable with certain aspects of time.

The one that you are most comfortable with will always have your focus. Similar to the precinct of service, your focus in this precinct will have a great deal of impact on your life. This precinct's three focus areas are immediacy, lifetime, and eternal.

Immediacy

When your perspective of purpose is obstructed, it will present itself in our relationship with time as an urge for immediacy in nearly everything. Because of your perspective, everything needs to come to fruition as soon as possible. You are most comfortable in and don't prefer using your resources unless results happen.

Everything in this neighborhood has to happen right now, or it isn't worth your time. Focusing only on what can serve you right now can be a block to many of the blessings you yearn for. As the old saying goes, anything worth having is worth waiting for. Things that hold value require time for their value to be revealed.

If you plant a tree, it takes time to grow. When a child is conceived, it takes nine months to be ready to come into the world. If your body is damaged, it can heal, but it only does so with time. Even with financial wealth, the longer you allow it to compound, the more it can grow. Some of the most incredible things in life only become accessible when your focus on time transitions out of immediacy.

In a society where everything is premised on high speed, it is easy to deduce how the need for speed in Western culture has affected our perspective of purpose. The danger of this precinct, the lowest of all three perspectives, is that you won't be *willing* to tap into your resources unless your *need for speed* is satisfied.

At this level, the moment you realize that an extended amount of time is needed for success, you won't put your resources into it. This focus can be lethal because, in life, the majority of things that have immediate gratification are passive suicide. All forms of immorality, escapism, and ill-pleasure are direct associates of immediate gratification. All of which are incredibly addicting and create a vice that binds you to its will.

Because of their addictive nature, you wouldn't dare use your resources at a high level for something else. Deep down, your mind knows that if you deplete your resources, pursuing delayed gratification, you'll never get to indulge in the many forms of evil associated with immediate gratification. It's a trap that you don't want to find yourself in!

Lifetime

Again, as your perspective of your purpose changes, you will see enormous shifts in your life. When you move from an obstructed perspective of purpose to one of Obscurity, your relationship with time changes. And as I stated before, you activate some of the best blessings in life when you can implore endurance, patience, and perseverance.

In this neighborhood, your perspective will shift your focus to a relationship with time that exits immediacy and enters a lifetime. This is where the focus shifts from immediate gratification to delayed gratification. If you see purpose from this angle, you start to use your resources for things that can last a lifetime or even a few generations. Business, life insurance, land, habits, etc., are on your radar.

I mentioned that things associated with immediate gratification are frequently associated with evil. If that statement is true, then the opposite must also be true. Things of delayed gratification are associated with varying types of good deeds. A quick analysis will show that this is true. Therefore, with this perspective comes an end to a life enriched with death and a new beginning of one rich with life.

Anything that creates and promotes life takes time. Your newfound focus creates life. You begin to give birth to new ideas, better habits, and stronger beliefs. Where life is, there is time also. If you take time away from life, death begins lurking in the shadows.

A tell-tale of someone who is in this precinct is consistency. The ability to display consistency over extended periods is vital. The ability to stick with things even when things are tough will show up in life.

Eternal

When you start seeing purpose from the observation perspective, your focus transitions its relationship with time into eternity. Your focus now shifts to principles, law, love, wisdom, and word. All of which are eternal.

In this precinct, the perspective of who you are meant to become is so clear that you become an immovable force. Nothing that shows up in life can alter your belief in who you are meant to be. In no way is this idea to be misunderstood for any form of being stubborn. It is meant to be seen congruently with the perseverance that presumes from being grounded and standing firm in Faith.

Due to the perseverance created from this perspective, no obstacle stops a person from accomplishing his or her purpose in life. An unbeatable resilience shows up. In the words of the late and great Viktor Frankl, "A person with a strong enough why can overcome any how."

The focus in this precinct is spirit-based. Spiritual things have been here since the beginning of time and will be here until the end of time. Operating with instead of against the wisdom, word, and principles of the Creator consistently works in your favor. It does so on levels we cannot understand within the realm of this life.

The Precinct of Sustenance

The third precinct is the neighborhood of sustenance. The focus in this precinct is what you believe gives you life. What is it that sustains your existence? You just can't see yourself living without what you focus on in this precinct. What do you believe is the primary source sustaining your life? The three perspectives shift your focus within this precinct in three ways: 1) Property, 2) Activity, and 3) Identity.

Property

From the perspective of Obstruction, your focus relative to sustenance is on property. Specifically, the tangible things that you own. Think materialistic. Apparel items, cars, a lovely home, jewelry, and the like are a few things that people with this perspective of purpose focus on. Not only are these things a focus, but they are also seen as what gives life.

The things that you own are what get you up and moving. Obtaining more property motivates you to pursue your goals and ideals. It's what makes you excited. If your property were to be taken away, life as you know it would cease. A trait of *actual* purpose is the joy that accompanies it. When your focus is here, you believe these things will give you the joy you yearn for.

The problem is when your perspective of purpose shifts your focus to material items, you expect the same emotional outcome as *your actual* purpose. This is why we see so many celebrities reach a certain level of stardom and riches and be in an atrocious mood. Some even go to the degree of performing drugs, committing suicide, overdosing, etc.!

You may say, "Well, how could someone with all that property feel so depressed or down?" Because, from this perspective, you see your life's purpose in the property instead of inside of you. Sometimes, we even view other people as being under our ownership. Spouses, children, siblings, and other close individuals are considered our own.

This is why we call them MY brother or MY wife and so on. In extreme cases, after these people die, someone may lose all sense of who they are and what they should do with their life. Again, this is because, at this level of perspective, we focus on property as our life's purpose. However, our property is not intended to nor can it replace your true purpose in life.

Activity

When your perspective of purpose moves from Obstruction to Obscurity, your focus in the precinct of sustenance also moves from property to activity. In this neighborhood, the things you do are what define you. Your perspective of purpose causes you to see what you do as your purpose.

Now, activity is vitally important. What you do is vital to your purpose and gives your life meaning. Although what you do is meant to be influenced by your purpose, it is not equivalent to it. When you see what you do as the equivalent of your purpose in life, it is a setup for failure. Why? Nothing on Earth is permanent.

Everything changes with the seasons of time. Therefore, when what you do has to change, you will become lost. For example, from an obscure perspective of purpose, it is easy to see your career as your purpose in life. What happens when your career is taken from you, you are laid off, fired, forced to quit, injured, or other unforeseen circumstances? If you can't be in that career field anymore, does that mean you no longer have a purpose in life? Of course not!

However, in Obscurity, this happens all the time in the sustenance neighborhood. Life is great until you can no longer do the activity you see as your purpose. What you do in life is not meant to be equal to your purpose in life. When your activity gives you life, when it is taken away from you, it will feel as though your life went with it.

Identity

Lastly, in the precinct of sustenance, your focus transitions to your identity. This only happens when your perspective allows you to observe your purpose. I love the analogy that Ed Mylett uses to describe identity. He says that identity is like a thermostat. Your core beliefs make up your identity. In simpler terms, the laws and principles you accept as "truth" determine the "degree" of your life.

If your thermostat is set to 70 degrees, it doesn't matter what happens in your external world, good or bad; you'll always find a way to bring your life back down to 70 degrees. You will naturally be around others who operate at the same temperature or around the same temperature as you. A perfect example is a lottery.

Let's say it takes a financial temperature of 200 degrees to maintain the winnings of the lottery. If, by serendipity, you happen to win the lottery, but your identity is only at 70 degrees, your thermostat will kick on the air conditioner to cool you off. Things in your imagination and your self-talk will reflect this, and you'll start doing activities that support your 70-degree identity.

The statistics support this analogy. Consider the lottery, where many winners spend their earnings prematurely, leaving them in the same financial position they were from the start. From this perspective, your focus must be on identity.

We were brought here to do work, and God clearly described the work we should be doing in the order it should be done. It looks like this: Be fruitful, multiply, replenish, subdue, and have dominion. The first instruction he gave was to BE! This is identity. Then he said to do three things that represent activity: multiply, replenish, and subdue. The last order was to HAVE dominion. This is property.

Therefore, our primary focus should be on identity. When you see your purpose in life as it should be, the only things that sustain you pertain to who you are. Everything else is secondary. As the author, David Hawkins, says in his best-seller Power vs. Force, "To be a success, it is necessary to embrace and operate from the basic principles that produce success, not just imitate the actions of successful people. To really do what they do, it is necessary to be like they are."

The Precinct of Sight

The last precinct is the neighborhood of Sight. The focus in this precinct is vision. You will begin to see a shift in personal resourcefulness as what you can see changes. Everything in this precinct is all about what you can see. How well can you see your purpose? The three divisions within this precinct are The Dark, The Fog, and The Light.

The Dark

From the perspective of Obstruction, your sight manifests as the neighborhood of darkness. From this perspective, you can't see anything. People who see purpose from this perspective are blind. They have no awareness of what they should have, what they should be doing, and, most importantly, who they are meant to be.

Their purpose does not impact them, and it directs their lives in no way. It isn't something that crosses their mind. Some don't believe they're here for any particular reason. They can't see what they like, what they're good at, or what moves them. Naturally, when sight is taken away, the other senses become heightened.

This causes extreme reactivity in their everyday lives. With no vision to guide them, their focus isn't on purpose but on their senses. Since all their energy flows to their senses, they react volatilely. What their eyes see, they have to have. What they smell creates a craving so intense it needs to be fulfilled. The slightest touch can create the wildest emotions. Sounds are exacerbated by an imagination flashing images of danger in the mind to survive.

The darkness is a scary place to be. When you are blind, your senses become your eyes. When you live your life from this perspective, the focus is always on your senses, and you are more than likely driven by fear.

The Fog

From the perspective of Obscurity, the precinct of sight shows up as the fog. Imagine walking into a neighborhood and seeing nothing but a thick cloud of fog covering it. You're able to see whenever you're in thick fog, but your vision is skewed. You become shortsighted. Lacking the ability to see afar, you can only see things close to your eyes. This causes your focus to be directly in front of you.

A while back, I was with my mom and my little sister driving down I-69, traveling to a little town called Anderson, IN. An extreme fog filled the air and limited my vision to only the tail lights of the car in front of me. In addition, the raindrops sounded like bullets as they fell upon the car's roof. With the windshield wipers screaming at me every tenth of a second and my speed reduced to a mere 40 MPH in a 70 MPH zone, I became laser-focused on the 20-30 yards in front of me that were visible.

This is what your sight is like when you view purpose from this perspective. Your vision is limited to what's directly in front of you. Everything else around you is unclear. It's obvious how the immediate situations in life impact you. Still, you have no idea how they'll impact you in the next 5 or 10 years. You may have a general idea of where you are going in life. But it lacks clarity. There is no vision for your life.

The Light

A few weeks ago, I was reaching around in the dark to find my glasses. The light switch was on the other side of the room, so I figured it'd be a waste of time to get up and turn on the light. I had to be on the floor, running my hands along the carpet for a few minutes. I couldn't seem to find them anywhere. After a few minutes, my daughter walked in, turned on the light, saw me on the floor, and asked me what I was doing. I told her, "I'm looking for my glasses." She laughed and said, "Dad, they're right beside you. Why didn't you turn on the light?"

When your perspective of purpose moves into Observation, you focus on having light in your life. It's like the moment my daughter flipped the light switch on for me. Everything becomes clear. You no longer feel comfortable operating in the dark or the fog. Suddenly, your focus isn't on the senses or directly in front of your feet. Your focus moves to your purpose in life.

It may take some time for it all to soak in. In other words, you may not understand everything instantly, but eventually, you'll become familiar with it. What used to be confusing and fearful makes more sense to you. You can make connections between past events in coordination with your purpose. You can examine it. A complete understanding of its main components is not impossible.

This is where you want your perspective to be *all* the time. The light comes with a realization of where your purpose in life has been. It comes with the realization that it's been within you the entire time.

Coach's Challenge: Now that you fully understand the model. Where would you be if you were to be dropped off into the state of purpose and you would be transported to the city that most resembled your life right now? Before you keep reading, stop to identify which precincts resemble your life the most. Maybe you'd be bouncing between cities to go to different neighborhoods? Or maybe you'd be living in Observation, where your crown is!? Only you can know the Truth. But don't rush past this section. If you can't remember all the precincts, take a second look at it. The point of this entire chapter is to provide you with a mirror that allows you to see your perspective clearly. Don't be afraid to look in the mirror. Whether you like what you see or not isn't important. What is important is that you raise your level of awareness to ensure you have the tools needed to create change.

The State of Purpose

Let's revisit the state of purpose. This state has three cities. In each city, different laws govern the land. Therefore, people think, act, and do things differently in each city.

In the city of Obstruction, they have their own perspective of why they are here. Obstruction is divided into four different neighborhoods. Each neighborhood is its precinct that is focused on something different. In Obstruction, the four neighborhoods are The Dark, Property, Immediacy, and Self. Clear across the state is the city of Obscurity.

The people who live in Obscurity also have their own perspective on how purpose in life works. The four neighboring precincts in Obscurity are The Fog, Activity, Lifetime, and Others.

The capital of the state is a city by the name of Observation. The people who make up its small populace have the only true perspective of how purpose operates. Because of their perspectives, the citizens of Obstruction don't believe that Observation exists, and the people of Obscurity search diligently for the road to Observation. Observation also has four precincts that make up its quadrant of neighborhoods. Its precincts are The Light, Identity, Eternal, and Humanity.

Can you imagine how the people's focus in the different neighborhoods would cause them to act? There is a law called the law of polarity. This law states that everything has two opposing ideas. This is a universal law. It applies to everything. I would like to pinpoint that the law of polarity also applies to your focus.

In life, there will always be situations. Some will be inherently good, and some will be bad. What will always remain true is that what you focus on will create more of it. When you focus on the good in a situation, you will get more of it. When you focus on the bad, you will get more of it.

What drives your focus? Your perspective drives your focus. That is why your perspective is so significant. When you *focus* on the obstacles in your life, you will only get more. But when you *focus* on turning everything into an opportunity, you will only get more opportunities. Your perspective of purpose determines your focus in life. In turn, what you are focused on will determine your experience in life.

Chapter 4 Summary:

- Perceptions are one of the most central themes in our lives. They are like a pair of glasses in that they influence our ability to navigate and understand life. Putting on a pair of glasses that aren't aligned with your vision will distort your ability to see and function properly. It is the same with the perspectives in our minds.

- Essentially, three lenses allow you to perceive life differently: 1) The Blindfold, 2) Drunk Goggles, and 3) Prescription Glasses. Having the right perspective can reveal rather than discover one's purpose. Your purpose is inherent but may be obscured by the lens through which it is viewed

- Each of the previously mentioned lenses represents you walking through life with one of three perspectives—Obstruction, Obscurity, and Observation—equated to distinct cities, each with four precincts representing neighborhoods. Each neighborhood has different focuses that manifest in the many domains of life.

- The four precincts of service, span of time, sustenance, and sight all manifest differently in our lives based upon which perspective we operate from. For example, your *service* will show up as favor for Self in the perspective of Obstruction. But your service will show up as favor for humankind from Observation's perspective.

- Obstruction is divided into four neighborhoods or precincts: The Dark, Property, Immediacy, and Self. Obscurity consists of four precincts: The Fog, Activity, Lifetime, and Others. And, of course, the capital, Observation, has four: The Light, Identity, Eternal, and Humanity.

- Understanding this analogy is a great way to shed light on how your perspective of your purpose shapes your life. It is a great tool to create awareness of where you currently are.

CHAPTER 5

THE POTENTIAL:

How To Remove All Limitations And Unlock Unlimited Potential

"You cannot live beyond the limits of your beliefs."

– *Myles Munroe*

"Your only limitation is in the confidence you place in what you perceive to be reality."

– *Robert Kiyosaki*

Recognizing & Removing Limitations

I f the perspectives of purpose were about focus, the domain of purpose is about recognizing and removing limitations. This section will cover four topics of discussion that will come together to reveal your potential:

Part One: The Purpose You Choose Determines the Dimensions of Your Purpose.

The purpose you choose to place at the center of your life can create boundaries. Or it eliminates all boundaries. Limitations are placed into your life whenever you choose any purpose other than your designated purpose. Choose Wisely.

Part Two: The Dimensions of Purpose

This section is all about revealing the foundation of the framework. It provides a description of the dimensions and why it is crucial to have a multidimensional purpose. This section also reveals your domain as you use the scoring system to visualize the size of the domain. The Gap is also introduced.

Part Three: The Domain

After your dimensions are revealed, you can now see your domain and what the gap is within your domain. Your domain will show how much untapped potential you have. You will also learn what happens when *you choose* to operate within someone else's domain.

Part Four: The Space

Your space is a raw representation of the things you can do. Your space has three direct links: Activity, Actualization, and Authority. This is where your potential lives in a limited or limitless state. The more space you have, the more you can put your resources to use. The same is true in the opposite direction.

The dimensions are three of the components of purpose: Resilience, Range, and Recognition. These three dimensions reveal the domain you operate within. Everybody has their own domain.

A domain is an area of territory owned by a ruler. That domain will show the limitations, or lack thereof, in your life. This is a representation of your space.

Space is God's raw material that He's left for us to move about, create within, and have dominion over. Therefore, the potential of your purpose is what disables you from or enables you to increase, fill up, control, and ultimately have dominion.

The purpose of this exercise is for you to assess how purpose is manifesting in your life right now. You want to identify what purpose is manifesting in your life. You want to take an assessment of how you currently use your resources. Everyone has already chosen a purpose to place on the mantle. Do you know what that is in your life? This is about figuring out what's currently there and making a change or being okay with what's already there.

The Purpose You Choose

We all have a choice! Your choice is based on your perspective of purpose. Within each perspective are infinite *purposes* available for you to use. *Whether you realize it or not, we have all chosen a purpose to be at the center of our lives.* It may or may not be the true purpose of your life.

The fact remains that there is a dominating and overarching theme in your life at this very moment. *You have chosen* that purpose from the options available within the boundaries of the perspective you operate from. Hopefully, by now, you've realized which perspective that has been for you.

Now, it is time to identify the purpose that currently governs your life. Then, you can decide to live with that or transition to your life's true purpose. Regardless of the central aim that currently exists for your life, it doesn't have to stay there. But if you want it to, then by all means, continue with life as is.

If you choose to leave your life as it is, this model can still serve as a helpful way to see if that purpose is empowering you or hindering you. However, I suggest you change it as we go through the rest of the material. In that case, you will reveal your true purpose, which can replace the replica you've been using. You can then return to the potential of purpose framework and reveal the potential within your purpose.

Choosing A Purpose

There are three distinct places that our purpose in life can come from. It can come from someone else; we can conjure one up or receive the purpose the Creator has prepared for us.

If You've Chosen a Purpose from Someone Else...

If it comes from someone else, it can come from many places. Those blessed enough to have parents alongside their journey may have been privy to preconceived ideas that shape their chosen purpose. Even extended family can have a large enough influence to implant thoughts that can grow and shape your perspective of your purpose.

Those present in our upbringing can often hand over to us the very purpose they feel they should have personified but didn't dare to pursue. Many of us have heard of the family businesses that generations have put so much into. This, too, can create such intense pressure in a person's life that it impels them to pick up the business and use it as their own purpose in life.

Even a dream career can often be the purpose many long for. Often, someone will be willing to offer you a "purpose" in exchange for using your resources. For example, you give an employer time and your body (physical labor), and they'll give you a purpose and meaning in exchange. In such instances, the company's mission may become the item you'd choose as your life's purpose. Usually, it winds up draining you of your resources and leaves you out to dry. This usually applies to people who have an obstructed view of purpose. Since they can't see their own, they'll take whatever is offered to them.

I don't want you to take this to mean that being in a supportive role is derogatory. There is nothing wrong with supporting another person in their endeavor. Some people are *meant* to play a supportive role. If this is true for you, then that is okay! You just need to be sure you are meant for a supportive role and aren't settling because of fear.

Be sure you aren't becoming what best-selling author Julia Cameron refers to as a *shadow artist*. A shadow artist is someone whose fear and doubts won't allow them to step into their true greatness, so they settle for a supporting role to live through someone else's greatness. They lurk in the shadows as supportive characters, but deep inside, a void has taken root in their heart.

Whether you do so with or without awareness, choosing your purpose in life from the options someone else gives you is dangerous. It doesn't necessarily mean it is a bad thing. It just poses a lot of risk. It must be done with extreme caution if you choose to do this (or have done so in the past).

The effects of choosing a life purpose that doesn't truly belong to you are detrimental. We will discuss the consequences in further detail in a few moments. But for now, we must be careful because another person's perspective can become our own.

Faith is produced by hearing. You may have heard the wrong things and are unaware of the fallacies. Was the purpose you've chosen given to you? Was it given to you by a person of good character and judgment? Is it truly your life's purpose? These may be tough questions, but they *must* be answered if you choose your life's purpose from the options another person has given you.

If You've Chosen a Purpose You've Created...

If you choose a purpose you have created, it can also come from various sources. Many beliefs given to us are so deeply implanted that we create dreams from them. The dream can feel so real that you believe it has to be yours.

If those beliefs are not "Truth," the dream you conjure up may not be meant for you but for another soul. For some, the desire to be loved by and have the approval of parental figures is so strong that we'd do anything for it. In my late 20s, I discovered that everything I was aspiring to become was simply for the love and approval of my father.

Through much meditation and self-searching, I discovered these intense feelings revolving around my father. My father used to be a musician. Growing up, I always wanted to be involved in music. I could play several instruments, write, and produce music at a young age. I gravitated towards it around seven years old because I was always around it. By the time I was 16, I had become really good at it. But when my dad stopped his journey in music, naturally, I stopped, too.

When it was time to go to college, I attended Purdue University for their Electrical Engineering. Years later, I found an old writing assignment from high school. Apparently, during my father's time working at a hospital when I was younger, I noticed on his badge he had the title "Engineering Technician."

There I was...in my early 20s, reading this writing assignment from years prior that stated, "I am going to go to college and become an engineer just like my father." I had no recollection of actually writing that...ever! When it came time to declare a major, I had no recollection of my father's "Engineering Technician" badge.

In my mind, I decided to become an engineer because I thought it suited me. But as I stood there reading this old paper, in my imagination, I could see a flash of the memory of my father's badge. It wasn't until later that I realized how much that moment during my childhood influenced my decisions as a young adult.

Through deep inner reflection, I realized that many of the things I had been doing in my life were for my father's approval. Some people even want to choose something opposite to their loved one's wishes as an act of independence. Nevertheless, unbeknownst to me, the purpose I had conjured and chosen for my life was to gain my father's approval.

I know many other people have similar circumstances. Their situation may appear as the pursuit of respect, love, wealth, esteem, survival, or many other human needs at the root of the world's deepest desires. You must be willing to do the inner work to weed out the mirages from the real thing. The inner work will reveal who you really are. Especially if you've chosen to create a purpose for your life. There is nothing wrong with this choice.

However, you need to do some serious work getting to know yourself to be sure you don't end up chasing a rabbit your entire life. Doing the inner work is the only way to discover if the purpose that's currently running your life is truly meant for you. This is the only way to know if you have created something custom-made for your identity or created something from your world's influence to satisfy the false self.

Receiving Your Purpose from a Higher Source...

The last source you could receive your purpose from is a source that exists outside of you and any other human. A personage that is invisible to the human eye. The Creator and Sustainer of all that is and will ever be. He sends the message of your life's purpose as a call within your spirit. Many of us block the call with inaction, fear, doubt, shame, worry, etc. All of which are created from our erroneous beliefs and misunderstanding of the laws we choose to cling to.

Some are so loud they block out the message on the other end of the call. Many are not willing to take the time to turn down the volume of the shouts of inaction, fear, doubt, shame, and worry. They'd much rather stay stuck viewing purpose from an obstructed *perspective*.

These are three options of where your purpose in life can come from. Remember that this is a choice that everyone has *already* made. Many people have made the choice without any awareness of doing so. The good news is that if you are reading this, you also have the *choice* to shift your perspective of purpose and choose a purpose from a perspective of observation.

The perspective you view purpose from will determine the boundaries you operate within. The awareness, or lack thereof, of your purpose, will create the limits of your reality. Whichever of the three sources you choose your purpose from, that purpose will determine your potential.

You must understand the significance of the choice of perspective and, ultimately, your life's purpose, which everyone makes, consciously or unconsciously. Once someone chooses a particular perspective, that perspective will lock them into a threshold of potential. Lower levels of potential will be associated with a lower-level perspective of purpose.

The same will be correct in the opposite direction. This means that only from an observative perspective of purpose can you experience the unlimited *potential* of your true purpose. Suppose you have an obstructed perspective of purpose. In that case, the only purpose you can see in your life will have little potential. You can be a prisoner in a domain someone else provides for you or a sovereign ruler in the domain the Creator has designed for you.

Within each perspective, there is an infinite number of combinations below a certain threshold. To increase your potential, you must change perspectives. Then and only then can you tap into a higher threshold of possibilities. In this way, your perspective and chosen purpose determine your potential. Choose well, and you can live a life without limits. If you choose wrong, you could be limited for a lifetime.

But when we choose, we have to live with the consequences of that decision, good or bad. God says he places life and death before us...we have to choose. In addition, to stand by idle and make no decision at all is equivalent to choosing death. There is no in-between. Indecision is the same as opposition.

> **Coach's Challenge:** This is an excellent time to pause and reflect. Take your time with the book. Really take the time to see yourself in the pages. What have you chosen to sit on the mantle of purpose in your life? Be honest with yourself. Reflect on where it came from. When did you choose it? Are you comfortable with it being there?

The Dimensions of Purpose

The dimensions are three distinct characteristics of purpose: 1) Range, 2) Resilience, and 3) Recognition. Together, they reveal your domain's limits or lack thereof. Just as the dimensions of a 3-dimensional shape (Length, Width, Height) reveal the bounds of its area, the dimensions of purpose (Range, Resilience, and Recognition) will reveal the bounds of your domain.

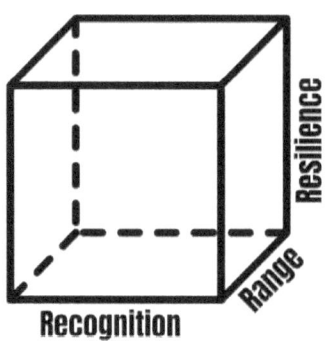

Range

The range of your purpose is the dimension that dictates how many areas of your life are affected by the purpose you have set as the dominant theme of your life. The Core 5 areas of your life, which we'll discuss in detail shortly, are Faith, Fellowship, Finances, Fitness, and Fruitfulness.

Anything you can do on this side of life can fall under one of these 5 keystones. If your range scores lower, your purpose will impact none or a few of The Core 5. If you have a healthy range, your purpose in life will affect every one of The Core 5.

Resilience

Resilience is the amount of perseverance and power your purpose will allow you to apply to The Core 5. This is especially true in the face of adversity. The more resilient you are, the more likely you'll be to endure the hard times you'll face. Notice the two different components of resilience: power and perseverance.

A resilient purpose is powerful and perseverant. This means that it will impact high levels of strength with your Core 5 and will do so through any obstacle or tribulation. A purpose lacking in this area will be short-lived and have little effect on your life.

For example, imagine a purpose with a strong range but weak resilience. It will be present in various aspects of your life. However, your purpose will have little influence over your thoughts, emotions, and actions. In addition, outside influences can and will easily overpower what little influence it presents.

Recognition

Lastly, there is recognition. This refers to your ability to consciously recognize when your life's purpose is present. When recognition is stronger, it grows from mere awareness into a sharp focus. When you are focused on the presence of your purpose in life, your recognition is taken to new heights.

When a purpose is recognized at the level of focus, it supports more efficient resource allocation and positively influences supportive behaviors. In terms of resource allocation, when you are focused on the presence of your purpose, it can serve as a prompt for you to tap into your resources.

When you know what needs to be done, you can use resources more efficiently. The use of resources will naturally influence your behaviors. If you are efficient with your resources, your behavior will support your purpose at higher levels. As the dimensions come together, your potential will be revealed. Each dimension will play a different role in your life.

A Conversation with The Creator

What if you got the chance to have a meeting with The Creator? In this meeting, He mentions that you can have any life you want. The only requirement is to show up at a different location the next day. As requested, you arrive bright and early the next day at the location you were provided with.

You open the door to a mysterious-looking room. As you take a step inside, you look to your right. The first thing you notice is The Creator standing there behind what looks like a control center. The control center is full of hundreds of controls far beyond your knowledge.

However, you notice a small screen with three columns labeled R in the console's center that says "*purpose*" below it. Above the small screen is an outline in the shape of a square. But the center of it is empty. Almost as if something is supposed to be placed in it.

You see a large shelf next to the control center with three columns going from the floor to the ceiling. But as you look up at the ceiling, you notice it's so high you can't tell where it ends. You see three golden nameplates on the floor at the threshold where each column begins. From left to right, they read Obstructed, Obscurity, and Observation.

Looking back at the columns, you observe that the obstructed and obscurity columns are empty. The observation column has one golden cube with your initials on it. You look at the Creator, and he's smiling. With delight, he says, "Pick up the cube."

Rolling the cube around in your hand, you see that three of its six sides have the letter R. Each letter has an infinity sign beneath it. You take a second to look up from the cube to see the other side of the room. There isn't much but a dark space. There is enough light to see a few feet in front of you, but further than that, it's too dark for you to make out how large the room is.

You hear The Creator's voice again, "Toss me the cube". The cube has some weight to it. So, your immediate thought is that the cube must be pure gold. You then toss the cube to the Creator. He puts the cube inside the square outline you saw on the control center.

As he places the cube in the control center, the lights in the room brighten up what looks like a dark and creepy room. That tiny screen in the console's center with the three Rs shows the same three infinity symbols on the cube.

You look up from the console, and that dark area of the room that you couldn't make out is completely lit. What the light reveals is an infinitely large cube. The cube is so large that you can't see where its boundaries end. The Creator steps out from behind the console and walks you to the cube.

The both of you step into the cube. As you stand at the edge of the cube's corner, your vantage point allows you to take in how massive the space is. What appears to be an endless white space occupies your attention. You look behind you and see that the front of the console the Creator was standing behind has a large screen with those same three Rs and the three infinity symbols.

He explains, "Those Rs you see create the dimensions of the space you are standing in. This space represents the potential that you have access to. Each "R" represents one of the dimensions of purpose. Only your true purpose in life can unlock the unlimited amount of potential that lives within you. Any purpose from the observation perspective will have the same limitless nature. Any purpose chosen from a perspective of obscurity or obstruction will limit what you can do. Your perspective is the very thing that can hold you back in life. Choose your perspective wisely!"

He continues, "The three columns of seemingly infinite-sized shelves over by the entrance represent the three perspectives of purpose. Before you grabbed *your* cube, you didn't notice any cubes on the other two shelves, did you? With a confused look, you politely tell him, "There are no cubes on the other two shelves."

The Creator smiles and continues, "This is because you will only *notice* options for your purpose in life within your chosen perspective. Those who see purpose from an obstructed perspective can only see cubes inside the obstructed column. If you had an obstructed perspective of your purpose in life, you would've only noticed the infinite number of cubes within the "obstructed" column of the shelf. The other two columns of the shelf would appear to be empty.

Also, instead of the infinity symbol beneath the Rs, every cube would have had different sets of numbers. Each number would be a representation of the limits that would be placed upon your potential. Smaller numbers mean less potential and bigger numbers mean more potential. To increase your space, you must change perspectives. You can be a prisoner in a limited space someone else provides you or a sovereign ruler in the unlimited space God has designed for you.

Within the perspectives of obstruction and obscurity, there is an infinite number of purposes beneath a certain threshold of potential. But within the perspective of observation, you will only see one purpose for your life. You will only see the purpose custom-tailored for *you*! Since you chose to see purpose from an observative perspective, you only saw one purpose and now have unlimited space.

The dimensions of your purpose in life come together to create your domain. A domain is an area of territory controlled by a ruler. This cube that you see is your domain. You are the sovereign ruler of this space. This is your field of activity, authority, and actualization. Inside of this domain is space. The space is a representation of potential. Everything created in your domain will be because you put it there."

The Creator then reaches into his pocket and hands you 5 small cubes. "What are these?" you ask. He responds, "These are your Core 5. Anything is possible with The Core 5 if you believe. Since you have unlimited space, your Core 5 can be as large or small as you desire. If your space was restricted, so would be your potential to do as you wish with your Core 5."

This is what the Potential of Purpose framework is envisioned to be.

Having a Multidimensional Purpose

So far, we have established that the perspective that you choose to have will determine what you can see as your purpose in life. You have been given the power to choose your purpose in life. However, you can only choose from the options your perspective will allow you to see.

Your choice of purpose will come with dimensions that indicate the potential that you will have in your life. That potential will either give you limitations or create a limitless environment in your mind. The potential that your purpose creates is an expression of what you can do in your life. Since this is true, your life's purpose needs to be multidimensional.

Consider how much potential was at your fingertips when you were inside the cube with The Creator. There was an infinite amount of space without limitations. That happens when your life's purpose is infinite in *every* dimension (Range, Resilience, and Recognition). But how would the potential be impacted if one of the dimensions had minimal strength?

Let's say that resilience, range, and recognition each represented the cube's length, width, and height. How much would the space you could access be impacted if you didn't have enough room to move about and accomplish what you envision for your Core 5? How would the capacity of the box change as you lost strength in one, two, or all three dimensions of purpose?

A multidimensional purpose holds a massive advantage in increasing your capacity to operate. The more multidimensional your purpose is, the more potential you will unlock. You can do more in your Core 5 when you unlock more potential.

For example, remember when being a flat earther was cool? This was around the time that everyone thought the Earth was *two-dimensional*. Having the *perspective* that the Earth was only two dimensions placed limits on their lives. They believed they would fall off the Earth's face *if they went too far*. The dimensions are like that.

The more multidimensional your purpose is, the fewer limitations you will create for yourself in your mind. To have multiple dimensions on a high level is to break free from limitations. The dimensions help you tap into more resources and allow you to use them for extended periods. The better and extended use of resources removes barriers that would otherwise limit your growth.

Another reason it is crucial to be multidimensional is because of energy. The amount of potential that you have available to you is directly proportionate to the amount of energy you have available. Have you ever used those generic batteries that come with a TV remote control? They don't last very long. Realistically, they won't last one day if you try to use them for something bigger than a remote control. The batteries only have the energy to serve *one* function with extreme *limitations*.

When your purpose isn't multidimensional, your energy is like that set of generic batteries. The energy a one-dimensional purpose will provide won't be enough to tap into the potential of your resources. Using the six resources that everyone was given takes energy. And you will need *massive* amounts of energy if you want to take *massive* action. You can only use one or a few of your resources when you have no, low, or poor energy. Not only that, but you will only be able to use those resources for a short time.

Using the God-given purpose designed for you is like using a solar panel that gets energy from the Son and never runs out. A solar panel gets its energy from an unlimited source of power. But a *manmade* power source holds limited potential. When you reveal and use your *true* purpose in life, it will be infinite in all three dimensions. The potential that the dimensions of your true purpose will unlock comes with a boost in energy from an unlimited source.

Viewing Your Domain

A domain is the area of territory controlled by a ruler. When all of the dimensions of your purpose in life come together, they create an area controlled by a ruler. This is the domain that you are operating in. However, there are a few more things that I want to bring to light regarding your domain.

Operating in The Wrong Domain

I mentioned earlier that those who don't know their purpose in life will often take any purpose offered to them. This usually happens because somebody else sees more value in the power of your resources than you do. So, you take the purpose offered to you and use that as your life's purpose. That purpose will create extreme limitations in your life.

In addition, every domain has a ruler. You aren't operating in your domain when you choose a purpose somebody else offers you. In this case, you must operate in *their* domain, where they are the ruler. No other human can offer you a purpose in life that matches the potential within your *true* purpose. This is part of the danger of choosing a purpose that isn't your *true* purpose.

You have a domain that *you* are responsible for. You are responsible for activating that domain with your life's true purpose and having dominion within it.

How The Core 5 Fit into Your Domain

Your Core 5 can become whatever you'd like them to be. But there's one big catch. *You have to have enough space in your domain to hold what you envision for your Core 5.* If your chosen life's purpose doesn't unlock enough potential to power each of your Core 5, something has to be left out.

Your energy, potential, and resources will be limited. The items in your Core 5 that are of less priority regarding the purpose you've selected will be left out. This is a big problem. They are called the *Core* 5 for a reason. You need *all* of them to have real success in life. You can't leave any of them out if you want true happiness.

I've been mentioning The Core 5 frequently, but up to this point, I've only provided a very brief description of them. Let's talk a little more about The Core 5!

The Core 5

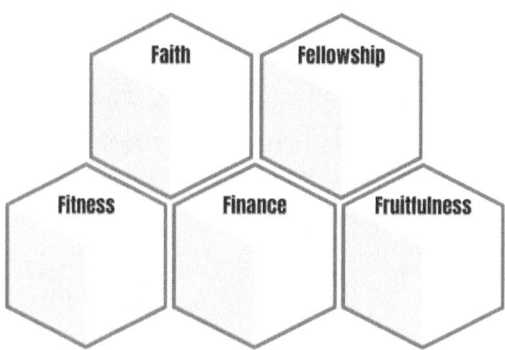

The Core 5 are the 5 subdomains you are responsible for within your area of dominion. The 5 are as follows: Faith, Fellowship, Finance, Fitness, and Fruitfulness. A domain is an area or territory owned and controlled by a particular ruler. That means that you are the sovereign ruler of these domains in your life. You get to dictate how they are played out.

Faith

The first of The Core 5 is faith. This subdomain dictates who, what, and how you believe. It is the foundation of everything that brings significance to your life. A person of little faith will have little meaning and direction in the other subdomains.

Faith isn't primarily about religious affiliation. I'm sure the first thing you thought of when you read "faith" is a religious affiliation. But this is the least in the subdomain of faith. At its core, it's really about what you *wholeheartedly* believe in.

Your faith is housed in a noun (person, place, or thing). You either have your faith here or there. No one is totally void of faith. Some people place their faith in good things, and some place their faith in bad things. Everybody believes in something. We choose to believe in some story that resonates with us.

It isn't a mystery why those of great faith are usually also of great accomplishment. In addition, those who are in great doubt are also usually in great stagnation. What do you believe regarding yourself, others, and the world? Is your belief housed in faith or housed in doubt?

How does all this relate to purpose? Whatever you choose to have at the center of your life (purpose) will dictate where you place your belief. Those whose purpose is blocked do not see the need to house their belief within faith. Their faith can stay in doubt, and they'll be content with their life remaining unchanged. You can't be bothered by not reaching new heights you don't even know exist.

Those whose purpose is obscure will be in between faith and doubt. They will have some beliefs of faith and some of doubt. Having a form of godliness but denying the power thereof. But there are always a select few individuals with a clear and distinct view of their true purpose in life. It's almost as if their vision forces them to have faith in what they see in their mind before they can see it in person.

They are fully convinced that what lives in their mind is the Truth. You couldn't tell them anything otherwise about the subject. That is true faith. Obstruction only believes what they see in person. Obscurity is torn between what they see in their mind and what they see with their eyes. But observation is convinced of what they see with their mind's eye.

So, in this sense, purpose directly affects what happens in this subdomain by shifting your belief from the external to the internal. But again, we are in control of what happens here. You have the choice to choose what you believe in. Choose wisely.

Fellowship

The subdomain of fellowship is all about the relationships with people we associate with. Our fellowship with others will fall into one of three categories: Family, Friendship, or Foe. Again, we are in direct control over this subdomain, just as all the others!

I know it's cliché, but I have to say it anyway, "you are the sum total of the five people you spend the most time with." In most cases, these are the people in our family. This is true whether it is close family or distant relatives.

This subdomain consists of the people we choose to have in our lives. Our family members are usually tied to us by blood. But the funny thing is that blood may bring life in the physical world, but belief brings life in the spiritual world. Blood may be thicker than water, but beliefs are more powerful than blood.

Friendships are tied by a belief. Some friendships are stronger than others. Usually, the more beliefs you have in common, the more robust the ties of friendships become. You may be thinking, "What about my associates?". Or even your colleagues at school or work. They are still friends but hold on by a thin thread of belief.

For instance, let's say you work with someone. You are cordial but have absolutely nothing in common outside of working at the same place. You never hang out outside of work. That thin thread of belief that your mutual employer will provide you with a paycheck is the only thing holding you and your coworker together. After one of you leaves the job, you may never speak again. That thin thread of belief has been severed, and with it, the friendship.

And yet, there is still another category of fellowship. This fellowship is tied by doubt. Doubt is belief in an outcome that you don't want. If I believe someone will harm me somehow, that is still a belief. It is a belief in a negative outcome. That person then becomes a foe. However, in the friendship, you both believed in a favorable outcome. If someone is a foe, you both have a belief about the same outcome. But one of you believes the outcome is good, and the other believes it is bad.

The opposing views create conflict. The great book says, "How can two walk together unless they agree." Fellowship can still be had with a foe. So long as the opposing beliefs aren't "stirred up."

Under other circumstances, some people have a belief that they want to get rid of. Another person with a greater belief is usually sought after as a mentor. Until the greater belief is "imprinted" upon the mentee, he and the mentor will have the fellowship of foes.

It is dangerous for the mentor to spend ample time with the mentee until signs of their new belief surface. Otherwise, the mentee's beliefs run the danger of attaching to the mentor. This is why, subconsciously, many mentors are cautious about who they allow into their lives. Unless, of course, the mentor believes *wholeheartedly* in Truth.

Flawed beliefs are like cubic zirconia. But when one *wholeheartedly* believes in Truth, the belief is likened to a diamond. Their belief cannot be cut, scratched, or broken under extreme pressure.

Finance

The third subdomain is finance. In this subdomain, there are three options: 1) You work for finances, 2) You put your finances to work for you, or 3) Your finances work for you and the generations after you.

The biggest thing with this subdomain is understanding that finance isn't about money. It's really about management. Finance has to do with your management skills. In today's society, this is a big part of our lives. Not because money is the be-all and end-all but because money is the central part of how exchange happens in our culture.

Before currency was a widely accepted system, we had to rely on the barter system whenever we exchanged value. Today, we use a monetary representation of value in an exchange. That's all money really is. It is a representation of value. That's why the amount of money you have symbolizes the value you give to the world.

Finance, on the other hand, is how anyone manages their money. How many managers have you seen taking orders from the very people they work for? Suppose you witnessed a manager answering to and depending upon his employees for plans and direction. In that case, I'm confident you'd think he was a lousy manager! Well, this is one type of manager in this subdomain. *The manager that works for their money.*

Did you know your money was an employee you are supposed to employ? Now, initially, most people may be required to work for their money because their parents may not have left them enough cash to learn how to manage their employees. As a result, by default, you are forced to work for your money because you need better management skills.

The second type of manager puts their money to work *for themselves*. The last type of manager in this subdomain puts their money to work *for themselves and the generations behind them.*

I *really* want you to ponder the question, "How many managers have you seen working for their employees?". The play on semantics is beautiful. If you've ever had a job, you know this goes against the natural order of things.

What would you think if you showed up on the first day of work and, instead of putting you to work, the manager sat you down to talk? He tells you that he has an agreement with another company that forces him to trade his employees after hiring them so he can keep the lights on. So, he has to trade you to another company instead of putting you to work. Then, he has to go to work to get more employees that he can trade to keep the lights on.

What would you think of this manager and his business? Is his business model great? Is this how you run your subdomain of finance? Remember, the Creator said you can do as you wish with The Core 5. You have a choice. This is different from how the Creator told you to run it, but the culture has made this financial model the standard way of business.

Fitness

Fitness is all about health. This isn't just about going to the gym. Fitness encompasses every level of physical, mental, and spiritual health.

Your spiritual health is the foundation of your health. Are your core beliefs based upon Truth or lies? How strong is your faith, goodness, knowledge, self-control, perseverance, godliness, brotherly kindness, and love? Are these things grounded in Truth as well? Is your conscience the voice of Truth, or have you been feeding it with Lies? What attitude do you have?

Your mental health will be primarily determined by the condition of your spirit. You'll also have a healthy mind if you have a healthy spirit. Here is some food for thought. What is the dominating force in your life? Are you moved by emotions or The Truth? How strong is your intellect? Have you developed the mental muscle to be able to reason and understand? Have you strengthened your imagination through planning, creating, meditation, reading, and dreaming? Or have you significantly reduced your imaginative abilities with excessive use of entertainment? How strong is your awareness? Do you know what you want, like, and dislike? Do you know who you are? Do you know who you are supposed to be?

Your physical health is also a direct reflection of your mental health. People who are strong in intellect, will, and imagination have the tools to stick to a diet and workout regimen. Sometimes, sticking with a workout regimen for an extended period can even wake up the positive traits of the mind.

Being a fit person entails all three divisions of this subdomain. The stronger you are in all three makes for a stronger person. Many people are concerned with the physical body. As I mentioned before, even though it is necessary to keep your physical health strong, your spiritual health is the only thing that stays with you forever. A regimen and diet for your spirit is even more impactful than having one for your physical body.

Fruitfulness

Fruitfulness is the subdomain of growth and development. To be fruitful means to have the capability to produce. The more you develop, the more you can produce.

There are four areas of development in which we can reach mastery. The bottom level is the physical level. The next level is the emotional level. Above the emotional level is the intellectual level. The top level is the spiritual level.

In the physical level of growth, all things encompassing our physical world fall into this category. Put simply, it is anything that uses physical power. At this level, many skills are learned and able to be developed. Learning how to type, fly a plane, sail a boat, play a sport, etc.

At the next level of emotion, anything concerning the way we feel is in this area of development. This is emotional power. There are many different types of emotions. But development in this area is vital because if you don't control your emotions, they control you. Growth at the emotional level is all about emotional awareness and control.

After emotional power is intellectual power. Intellectual power is a beast of a level. While emotions hold significant power, they are often fleeting. Intellect has the power to connect with Truth. Information based on Truth creates opportunity and new possibilities. In addition, the implementation of that information creates transformations. To grow on this level is to allow new information to open your mind to new and higher possibilities.

At the top level is the power of the spirit. This is the power of belief. Information can only be implemented once it is believed. Belief is where implementation occurs. The cluster of beliefs we hold makes up who we are. At the top level of development is the growth or decay of identity. To grow at this level is to imprint belief in the Truth upon your subconscious. To reach mastery at this level is to become who you are meant to be.

Within each level of development, we can master its components for ourselves and others. This means that the components can be mastered individually. But after we grow into mastery on a personal level, we also can step into another realm of development. The next realm of development is helping other people master a level of growth in their own lives.

This entire subdomain can be seen as a garden split into four different sectors. Each sector represents one of the levels of development. You begin with one seed in each level of development. The more you care for a seed, the more it grows into a tree. When the tree has fully grown fruit, you have reached mastery for yourself. You are now able to eat from that tree. You will eventually become fruitful in abundance.

However, when you eat the fruit from the tree you've grown, it has a seed of its own kind inside of it. You can now grow more trees in that sector with the seeds from the fruit of the previous tree. When you grow more trees, people will notice and come to eat from the fruit in your area of mastery.

When they eat from your tree, that fruit bears seeds they can take back to their garden to cultivate. If they develop the seeds they received from your tree's fruit, then people can come to their garden and continue the cycle. It creates a revolving door of growth.

That is how the subdomain of fruitfulness works. Your growth and eventual mastery create growth for someone else. Then, their growth can create more growth for someone else. It becomes a never-ending cycle.

Coach's Challenge: *If you took the time to reflect on your current purpose, now is the time to reflect further. Your current purpose...are its dimensions (range, resilience, and recognition) strong enough to influence all of your Core 5? Consider all your Faith, Fellowship, Fitness, Finance, and Fruitfulness individually. How are each of the 5 being impacted by your purpose?*

A Goal vs a Purpose

Keep in mind that purpose is an overarching concept. This means that it supersedes The Core 5. From your purpose, you will develop goals and plans within each subdomain. Understand that your true purpose in life will <u>not</u> come from within one of The Core 5. Your true purpose will always be over your Core 5.

This is because your life's purpose acts as an activator for each of The Core 5 in your life. Your true purpose will activate goals, activity, actualization, and authority in your Core 5. If you chose the equivalent of one of your Core 5's goals as your life's purpose, it wouldn't have enough power to activate all the other subdomains. This is why they are *sub*-domains.

They are made to be *beneath* your purpose in life. If your life's purpose came out of one of The Core 5, then all the others couldn't be activated. The purpose in your life is meant to be above and over all your subdomains. Your life's true purpose is like an infinite well of energy, goals, activity, ideas, will, etc., that all your subdomains engage with to quench their thirst.

I bring this up because people often mistake the goals within The Core 5 for their purpose in life. However, goals do not constitute purpose *in life*. It is actually the opposite. Your purpose in life is the *cornerstone* of all the goals you create within The Core 5.

To take a goal in one of the subdomains and put it in the place of your purpose in life is to go against the natural order of things. It also creates lots of confusion and, repeatedly, even depression. Why? Goals are meant to be accomplished. What happens when the goal is accomplished? Then what? What was once your purpose is now complete, but your life continues. Life at that point would be seen as pointless. This is the danger of choosing a goal as your life's purpose.

I brought this up in the principles of purpose for this very reason. Meaning and purpose often need clarification. Recall that meaning has to do with a result, but your purpose has to do with a reason. The Core 5 are also *life's 5 areas of meaning*. Because the things that matter most to us will always come from one or even all of these 5 things.

However, The Core 5 is not the purpose of our lives. This does not mean the subdomains are any less significant than your purpose. They are just different. Purpose drives meaning, and meaning often reinforces purpose. Think of an archer's approach regarding ready, aim, and fire. Purpose is an aim. An aim cannot be accomplished. It is not an achievement. It sets an intention.

Meaning is the firing of an arrow. It is the significance behind the intention. It brings fulfillment or failure. The firing of the arrow comes and goes, but the intent is always to hit the bullseye. One isn't necessarily more significant than the other. Both purpose and goals play their role in the equation of success.

Your Space & Your Resources

In the analogy of the potential of purpose I used earlier, the Creator gave you your Core 5 and said you can do whatever you like with them. Your resources are how you bring into reality what you envision for your Core 5. In the analogy, the Creator didn't give you any resources because they are already in and around you. As a reminder, the six resources are Body, Mind, Spirit, Matter, Space, and Time.

Notice that one of the resources is the very thing that the domain you are responsible for controlling creates...space. How does that work? We can use each resource individually. However, we also can combine our resources and use them to create exponential growth. Time, space, and matter are representations of pure potential. Time is pure potential of who we can become. Space represents pure potential of what we can do. Lastly, matter is pure potential of what we can have. The other three resources (spirit, mind, and body) have tools that influence the potential they are tied to.

Spirit – Time

Mind – Space

Body – Matter

Your spirit is directly linked with time. Remember that time is pure potential for who we can become. A belief is your spirit's tool to tap into the potential within time. Time is what a belief needs to do its magic.

Next, the mind is tied to space. The tool that the mind uses to tap into the potential within space is thought. Thoughts are the original ideations used to represent how space can be manipulated. Nothing exists in space without first originating in the mind. Also, for the objects within your mind to manifest, there must be enough space to support the object.

Lastly, the body is linked with the potential that exists within matter. The tools the body uses to activate this potential are its bodily members. Primarily your hands. All objects made up of matter have to be created through a body. Whether the body creates a machine or does the physical labor itself, without the body, the potential within matter would lie dormant.

As you saw in the Principles of Purpose, these tools aren't the only tools belonging to the resources but are pivotal in releasing potential. That's how the resources work when they are linked together. They can also function independently.

The spirit holds all of our core beliefs. The situations that life brings to us will be "filtered" through these beliefs. After being filtered, we have a perspective about the situation in the form of ideas. These thoughts create emotions that influence what we do with our bodies. All of our ideas need time. Anything that will enter the space we occupy needs time. It also needs space to occupy. Lastly, it needs the molecules (matter) in the correct combination to occupy the space.

There isn't anything that has ever been created without these 6 resources. So again, the Creator didn't give you any resources because you already have everything you need. You just have to use them properly.

Limited Resources vs. Unlimited Resources

The only resource we have that is unlimited is our spirit. The other five resources are all limited. The body does not last forever and will eventually return to dust. Time can only exist within bounds. If time was released from its limits, it would cease to exist. Time cannot exist in eternity.

Space as we know it also has limits. While we have yet to learn just how expansive space is, one thing remains true. The amount of space we have access to is and will remain limited. Matter is limited. The Earth as we know it is being rapidly depleted of its resources.

And while the mind may be unlimited in nature. Like space, we really don't know of its limits. They tell us we only use a small percentage of the brain's power. But the brain isn't the mind. However, the mind can control the brain because the brain is the mind's resource through which it operates. So, while the mind may not be limited per se, its medium is limited. Therefore, in this life, it does have indirect limitations.

I say all that to point out that the only resource we know to be unlimited is the one that gets the least attention. Many people are willing to spend money, time, mind, and space on their bodies. How many people spend time building and strengthening their spirit just as they do their bodies? The most important work we can do is to develop our spirit and the spirits of others.

Finding The Gap

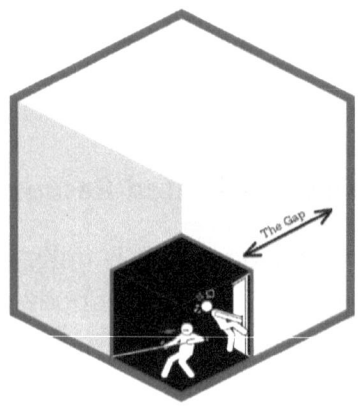

We have already established that your *true* purpose in life will be unlimited in every dimension. We are looking to assess the *present* purpose that is dominating your life. Once we do that, we can assess your present purpose to reveal its potential.

Doing this can provide many unanswered questions you may have had about your life. It can answer why, at times, it feels like you've been hitting a proverbial glass ceiling. Once you can see the difference between the potential of your *present* purpose and your *true* purpose, that vantage point will also reveal what I call The Gap.

The Gap is the difference between your present purpose's limited potential and your true purpose's unlimited potential. The first step is to reveal your present purpose.

Finding Your Present Purpose

You have to look at your resource allocation to find your present purpose. Your purpose will always dictate how your resources are distributed among your Core 5. Your resources are how you support or bring to fruition your chosen purpose. In this way, your purpose acts as a governor for your resources.

If you've chosen a career, money, respect, revenge, comfort, benevolence, esteem, approval, or anything else as the purpose for your life, all or the majority of your resources will be governed accordingly. You will deplete every drop of your resources to ensure your present life purpose is taken care of. This is why you first need to look at your resources.

To fully assess your resources, you need to document how you use all six of your resources every day for at least seven days. You can do it at night, periodically throughout the day, the morning after, or however you like. So long as you do this every day for at least a week.

You will be looking for how you use the tools of each resource I mentioned in the third principle of purpose: *You're Already Equipped For Purpose.* For example, for your mind, you will track how you use your thoughts, emotions, intellect, imagination, and free will. At the end of the seven days, you will have the raw material to reveal your *current* purpose.

Once you have at least a week's worth of documentation of your resources, it's time to put on your detective hat. The next step is to search through everything you have documented. You are looking for one thing: Conformity.

You are *only* trying to find the object, path, or desire that you conform your resources to the *most*. There is power in your resources. There is one outcome that you use that power for the most. You are willing to submit the power of your resources to get to that outcome. It doesn't matter if you submit the resource voluntarily or involuntarily. You will find that there are many things you submit your resources to.

What you want to look for is the person, organization, place, or thing that gets your resources the *most!* The outcome you will submit your resources to, even against your wishes and desires, for an outcome. It doesn't matter what emotion arises within your body because you will *still* submit your resources. That *one* thing is what you are looking for. Once you find it, you need to answer one question: *Why* am I willing to submit the power of my resources to get this outcome?

The answer to that question will point to what you have at the center of your life. That answer is the cube at the center of the console, determining how much potential you have. It is your life's dominating theme, whether good, bad, or indifferent. If you conclude that you don't have anything at the center of your life, then you are more than likely lost. You have yet to decide what to do with your resources, so you'll do whatever you *feel* like doing at any given time. You will be willing to go wherever your emotions take you since you have no clear direction.

If this is the case, that is okay. That is the reason you have picked up this book. In phase three, I'll show you some tools you can use to reveal who you are so you can better assess yourself after you've done some inner work. After this exercise, you can use the potential of purpose framework to discover your potential and the size of The Gap.

> **Coach's Challenge:** *If you want to make the most of this book, do the suggested exercises! So here is another challenge. For the next 7 days, wait to read further into this book. Only focus on the exercise I mentioned in the above section. Track all of your resources and see where they lead you! If you accept the challenge, you won't regret it!*

Finding The Gap

In the previous story titled "A *Conversation with The Creator*," I had you imagine that you picked a cube from the shelf of the perspectives of purpose. That cube was then placed into a control center that activated the potential of that purpose. In this section, we'll do something similar to your present purpose. When that potential is revealed, you can see the limitations of your present purpose. That will also reveal The Gap.

Each dimension of purpose will be scored based on parameters ranging from 0-8. The numbers 0,2,4 and 8 represent different thresholds of potential. The number 8 is the number of abundance. If you turn an 8 on its side, it turns into an infinity sign. That is why the number 8 is the highest on the scale. If you add up all the numbers from each dimension, they will reveal the domain that you are operating in. That domain holds the potential that you currently have access to.

This is how each domain can be scored relating to any *present* purpose.

Recognition

0 – No awareness of any purpose in life

2 – Awareness of *present* purpose in life

4 – Aware of their true purpose in life

8 (∞) – Focused on their *true* purpose in life

Range

0 – Influences none of The Core 5

2 – Influences one of The Core 5

4 – Influences more than one of the Core 5

8 (∞) – Influences all of The Core 5

Resilience

0 – No power or perseverance in The Core 5

2 – Power but no perseverance in The Core 5

4 – Little or no power but has perseverance in The Core 5

8 (∞) – Power & Perseverance in The Core 5

All of these can be scored within the potential of purpose framework inside a cube. The cube's edges would represent your life's true purpose and be scored with an infinity sign. The inner boundaries of the cube can be scored with your present purpose. As you connect the lines, it will reveal the limits currently being placed on your life. The Gap will also be revealed as you can see where you are and where you could be.

The Gap

When *true purpose* isn't accessible because of your perspective, you will be restricted to limited space. This means small amounts of resilience, range, and recognition in your Core 5. When what you can do in your life is limited, you simply won't be able to fit all the subdomains into your life. For example, when your finances replace purpose, you will need more resources to tap into your family and fruitfulness because you've spent all your resources on finance. Your potential is tapped out!

But what happens to the dimensions of your purpose when you tap into the power of *your true purpose*? The space becomes unlimited because your gift has made room for you. It will open up new opportunities and possibilities. When your dimensions are unlimited, your potential becomes unlimited in The Core 5.

Not only that, but your domain can have so much space that you'll have the energy to bring other people into your life and expose them to what you've done. You can bring other people into your dominion and show them how it is meant to be. We can bring healing to nations and end wrongful suffering for people. Think of someone like MLK. By tapping into his purpose, he was able to have enough "space" in his life to expose an entire race of people to the way things are meant to be. In this way, the activity you can perform dictates the impact you can have on the world.

This presents a problem. Currently, there's a purpose that you have chosen to be the dominant theme in your life. Let's say your present purpose is different from your *true* purpose. In this case, it'd create a discrepancy between the domain you currently operate within and the domain you can operate within. That discrepancy is space that you don't yet have access to. This space between the two domains is called *The Gap*. The Gap is a representation of untapped potential. When you reveal and function in your true purpose, you will unlock your untapped potential and fill the gap.

If you aren't using your *true* purpose as the center of your life, there will come a time in life when you experience a trigger that shifts your perspective. When that happens, you'll start to see the limits and boundaries that your "space" has placed in your life. This will cause dissonance between what you know you're capable of doing (the space you should have) and your current reality. Looking back at the shelf with 3 columns by the entrance, you'll see that the perspective you chose your purpose cube from is empty. One of the other two columns is now available. You have to switch out cubes. Only then will your life begin to change.

Chapter 5 Summary:

- EVERYONE has a purpose that is currently dominating their lives. One of the most meaningful self-assessments anyone can perform is identifying their *current purpose* and the source where it may have originated. One of the most important adjustments you can make is to align your current purpose with your true purpose. When you do so, that decision will be the one that unlocks your unlimited potential.
- The purpose we currently have sitting at the center of our lives can power growth in the many subdomains of our lives. Only our true purpose has the potential to touch and power *all* the subdomains of our lives. Living for any other purpose comes with its own unique limitations.
- We each have Domains that we were brought here to have dominion over. When your true purpose is activated, this domain becomes available. Also, your potential in your Core 5: Faith, Fellowship, Fitness, Finance, and Fruitfulness becomes unlimited.
- One of your most prominent goals in life should be closing the gap between your current and eternal purpose.

Getting ready for Phase 3

Before transitioning into phase three, let's summarize what we learned in phase 2.

The Prescription

The prescription was meant to give you a good look at the tip of the iceberg of the power your purpose holds. Once you reveal and embody your purpose, this power will be brought into your life. Remember, the big idea here was that your purpose unlocks health, wealth, and longevity.

The Pathways

Even though it's about teaching you the different paths you can take along your journey, the main point in this section was about the triggers. Everyone has triggers meant to wake them from their slumber in life. This is to get the journey on one of the pathways started. Recognize the triggers in your life and use them to your advantage.

The Perspectives

The perspectives were all about showing you how, as your focus changes, the things that manifest in your life do as well. Depending on your *chosen* perspective, the things in your life that you give your attention and resources to will change. Remember, your perspective will dictate what you see. What you see will control what you can focus on. Where your focus goes, your energy flows. Lastly, what you focus on is what you give life to. What are you breathing life into? If what you are bringing into your life doesn't match what you desire, check your perspective!

The Potential

The potential was all about recognizing and removing limitations in your life. Your perspective of your purpose in life is what dictates the limits you place or remove from your life. I wanted you to see that you don't have to operate in someone else's domain for your entire life if you don't want to. In addition, you have unlimited potential if you tap into and believe in your true purpose in life. You just have to choose your perspective carefully!

At this point, you should have a great foundation of the concepts and statistics of your purpose in life. At this point, you should understand what it means to have purpose. And you know the mindset required to live on purpose. Now, let's reveal your eternal nature!

PHASE THREE –
Revealing Purpose

Welcome to phase three! In this phase, we'll cover three core frameworks: The Revelation, The Blueprint, and The Filter. It's going to be like building a house. In The Revelation, we will build the home's foundation. In The Blueprint, we will put together all the internal and external pieces that go on top of the foundation: The roof, drywall, landscaping, furniture, décor, etc. After that, The Filter will be like having an inspector come out and look at the property to ensure it was built to the proper standards. Let's start building!

CHAPTER 6

THE REVELATION:

Why Your Purpose is NOT What You Do

Dharma — Your Eternal Purpose

Dharma is a Sanskrit word that is difficult to translate into English. In Sanskrit, it carries many meanings. For this lesson, we will use its meaning of "eternal purpose" or our "true nature." Do you know who you are?

This is not a question of name, age, height, skin color, or any other tag commonly placed upon our physical nature. I am referencing the true essence of who you are. Three layers make up who you are: The Body, The Mind, and The Spirit.

The Body

The lowest layer is the body. The layer of the body holds all of the physical traits and characteristics often used to identify who you are. This is *not* who you are. Instead, it is a temporary covering and vehicle of who you are.

For some people, this is the only layer of Self that's known and given attention. How tall you are, your complexion, hair color and style, eye color, fashion style, shoe size, and so forth comprise this layer of Self. It is the first thing you notice about someone but also the least important.

The Mind

Above the layer of the body is the layer of the mind. How you feel, your thoughts, your preferences, and your awareness of your environment exist in your mind. In Western culture, this is a big topic regarding dating. Some television shows, board games, and apps are dedicated to this layer of Self.

These things often come to mind when thinking of how well you know someone. All the "would you rather" type of questions often reveal who you are within this layer of Self. The common belief is that once you *know* someone, you will know all their favorites, preferences, and deepest desires. While this common thought holds some validity, even this level of Self doesn't display who you truly are.

The Spirit

At the top layer is the characteristics of your spirit. What you believe and your attitude. All the invisible characteristics that make up who you are live within your spirit. These are traits such as perseverance, goodness, kindness, grit, diligence, will, drive, desire, tenacity, forgiveness, self-control, love, and patience, to name a few.

At this level, it's all about your beliefs. There are two types of beliefs. There are major beliefs and minor beliefs. We all have thousands upon thousands of minor beliefs. Every minor belief is a result of a major belief. We won't have many major beliefs.

Your major beliefs are the root cause of every thought, feeling, and action you take. These beliefs become who you truly are as they take root in your spirit. The culmination of all three levels makes up who you uniquely are in this form. However, your spirit is the only piece of you that will accompany you into the next life. Therefore, it should represent a sacred temple you build with care and delicacy.

A word of caution before I go further into this section. I will be using the word dharma often in this chapter. The word dharma doesn't necessarily have to have any religious affiliation. Simply see it for what it is...a word. If the word dharma throws you off, simply replace it with the words "true purpose." Use a play on semantics to trick your mind into opening up. In most Eastern traditions, the word dharma is affiliated with the true nature of a person's existence. Not the purpose of an action but of existence. This is what I've been referring to as *your* true purpose.

Three components within your spirit unite to reveal your dharma. The three components are compassion (what the world needs, service, usefulness), passion (what you love to do, gift), and expertise (what you are good at, skill, talent). Where these three meet, your "dharma" is revealed. Consider each component to be directional arrows that point directly to your dharma. When you combine all three, you can better pinpoint your dharma.

Identity

There comes a point in every book that contains the key message. This is that point for this book. If you've been skimping through this material, now is the time to pay attention. If you don't get anything else from this material, I want you to understand this Truth! I've hinted at this a few times within this material. Are you ready? Here it is!

Your life's purpose is not a goal; it has nothing to do with your material possessions, and it is not to do a specific task. The purpose of your life is to be. This is why the first order humans were given was to "be"! The story says that after Man was created, the first thing God said to him was to "be" fruitful. To be fruitful means to produce. The word "be" means to exist.

There is a reason why our spirit is moved by our <u>be</u>liefs. I find it wildly ironic that, as a child, we were always focused on who we would <u>be</u>come. I am referencing that age-old question that kids get asked, "What do you want to <u>be</u> when you grow up?" That question seems to be reserved for children. For some reason, as we grow older, the conversation often moves to what we want to do.

No one ever asks an adult who they want to be. The question transitions to, "What do you do?" Who we want to become takes a back seat to doing *whatever it takes* to sustain life. It's almost as if when you become a *grown-up*, you're programmed to default to survival mode. As an adult, it doesn't seem to matter much who you are. As long as you can provide for yourself, who you are seems to be the least of your worries.

What we do is very important. However, prioritizing what you do over who you're becoming is like creating the foundation for your home with the material needed for building the actual house. Imagine pouring the foundation of a home with windows, siding, roofing, and drywall. Then, building on top of that. The mere thought of doing that seems absurd!

When a house is built, different materials are used for the foundation, the structure, and the furnishings/decor. If you were a home, the foundation would be who you are. The house itself would be what you do. The furnishing and décor would constitute what you have. Your priority should always be on the foundation.

Imagine you build a beautiful home with the best furnishings atop a weak foundation. Will it not be destroyed when tested by the forces of nature? It is the same when building your spiritual temple. The foundation needs to be your primary concern. Only then should you proceed to design and build your home.

All the most distinguished people who have been revered for centuries, or even millennia in some cases, all focused on their _being_. Moses was born to _be_ a Leader. Paul of Tarsus was born to _be_ a messenger. Abraham was born to _be_ a father. Jesus was born to _be_ a savior. Gandhi, MLK, and Mandela were born to _be_ liberators. Michelangelo was born to _be_ an artist. Isaac Newton was born to _be_ an observer. Thomas Edison and The Wright Brothers were born to _be_ inventors. Beethoven and Mozart were born to _be_ composers. William Shakespeare was born to _be_ a writer. Socrates was born to _be_ a thinker. Walt Disney was born to _be_ an Imagineer.

That list could be endless. To reap the benefits of _your_ dharma, your focus has to be on who you were born to become! The rest will follow. When you focus on who you should become, what you should do and have will follow suit. What you should do naturally flows out of your being.

Take Paul of Tarsus, for example. Paul was born to be a messenger, but his dharma manifested through writing, missionary work, and teaching. To be focused on what you should do without knowing who you need to become disturbs the natural order of creation. Out of your being flows your actions. Once you become who you were meant to be, your gifts will be the medium through which you create and produce value. This is part of why I've said that your passions and gifts will point toward your purpose.

Take note that your purpose cannot be accomplished. This is because your identity is not a goal. A goal is meant to be accomplished. Your dharma, on the other hand, is meant to be embodied. It is who you are, not what you have done.

When you personify your true nature, the things you create often become such a catalyst within the modern-day culture that who you are remains, through your production, even after your physical body has left this Earth. Sticking with the example of Paul, his books are still being read. All his teachings are still being taught even thousands of years after his physical body has passed.

Think about how many people were affected by the good works of the people previously mentioned. Martin Luther King Jr., Nelson Mandela, Michelangelo, The Wright Brothers, and numerous others still influence minds today. The good works that your true nature will produce will alter the lives of countless people for the better.

It wasn't only about their personal endeavors. Even though they may have received joy from their works, their creations were produced to uplift mankind. This is a small taste of the power of purpose. This is part of the power of your dharma.

Unlocking The Components of Your Dharma

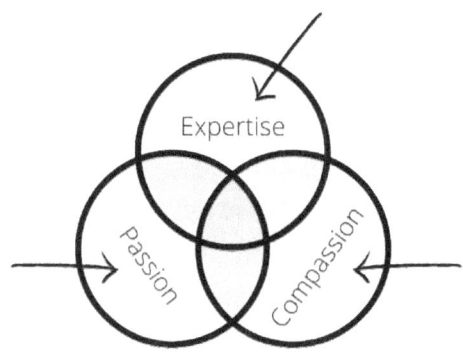

Before revealing your dharma, we must unlock the prerequisite doors of passion, compassion, and expertise. Your purpose will reveal itself once you know yourself well enough to see all three prerequisites clearly. We'll begin the prerequisites by unlocking your passions.

Unlocking Your Passions

Passions are a *feeling* of intense enthusiasm or a compelling *desire* for someone or something. There is a direct link between interest, attention, and passion. Allow me to give you a brief description of how these are related.

Gaining Interest

Passion and interest are directly linked to one another. Your interests are the forerunners of your passions. At a certain point, if an interest continues to grow, it will develop into a passion. An interest is like a seed. If you plant it in the right environment and give it what it needs, one day, it will blossom into a passion.

Now, how does attention fit into this equation? Attention is a byproduct of interest. If your interest is lacking, your attention will be absent. When you are wildly interested in something, you can *pay* more attention. In this sense, attention can literally be seen as a currency.

Not only is attention like money, but as your interest reaches higher levels, it pays out with attention of higher quantity and quality. The four different kinds of attention are divided, alternating, selective, and sustained attention. As interest grows, we are able to *pay* more attention and do so with better efficiency. Continuing with the finance theme, it may make the analogy easier to view attention as a literal profit.

In finance, if you gain interest in an investment, you also gain a profit. Consider attention to be the profit that you gain as your *interest* increases. The more interest you have in a topic or person, the more attention you'll have to spend.

This can be likened to an investment. Interest pays you with attention. Then you literally *pay with attention.* You take the attention and put it back into the interest account. The attention causes the interest account to grow even more. The higher interest account will produce even more attention. It becomes a constant cycle where interest and attention feed each other until the interest develops into a passion.

As you garner and spend more attention, the combination of interest and attention exudes specific characteristics. These are spelled out perfectly in the classic book "Flow" 6. The author, Mihaly Csikszentmihalyi, says 8 distinct characteristics of flow are associated with enjoyment: Complete concentration, clear goals, immediate feedback, alteration of time, concern for the Self disappears, effortless involvement w/o rumination, challenge & skill meet head-on, and a sense of control over all actions.

Passions come with intense enthusiasm and compelling desire because of the enjoyment of being in flow. The most common sign of flow is the illusory nature that time takes on. We've all looked at the clock after finishing an activity and said, "Time flies when we're _____ ___." Did you finish that sentence with "having fun?"

Another Word of Caution

The _big_ caveat is the illusory trance of pleasures I mentioned in the section on the pathways to purpose. You must be able to differentiate between a pleasure and a passion. Some of the strongest curiosities are the ones that draw us closer to the pleasures of the world. These curiosities will lead to a purpose, just not the purpose that you were destined to embody. So, tread carefully in the waters of what you believe to be passions.

If an activity or a person becomes a form of escapism, slavery, or strife, it is probably a pleasure and _not_ a passion. When escapism is rampant in your desires, you are merely seeking to escape the realities of your life. You'd rather be in a different "dimension" than continue living in what you have attracted into your life.

Slavery is indicative of the control the activity or person steals from you. When this happens, you become a slave that answers to your pleasure's every beck and call. The slavery mindset may also present as an extreme attachment. Even to the point that you feel you can't live without it.

The strife refers to the conflict it creates in your life. The out-of-control nature is associated with a constant demand that cannot be fulfilled. Also, be reminded of the characteristics of a passion: giving, freeing, advancing, upright, and disciplined. I repeat this information to reiterate its importance with the things you deem to be a passion.

Looking for your passions is a great help toward finding the things that put you in a flow state. As your interest grows, your attention payouts will transition into flow states. You'll find that when you _pay_ attention, it begins to be associated with the eight characteristics of flow I mentioned earlier. But this is a gradual process.

The 4 Phases of Interest Development

Education Psychologists K Ann Renninger and Suzzane Hidi have developed a model titled "The Four Phases of Interest Development" 12. The model powerfully illustrates how an interest grows into a passion over time.

Within "The Four Phases of Interest Development" model, these brilliant women break the process into four phases: 1) Triggered Situation Interest, 2) Maintained Situation Interest, 3) Emerging Individual Interest, and 4) Well-Developed Individual Interest.

The first two phases are based on a situation. This means that the interest may not be a personal interest. There will be something in life that is presenting itself to you that _forces_ you to engage. This can be because of a school assignment, health condition, social injustice, work requirement, relationship, or many other things that influence your life. The point is that the interest isn't yours. The interest is only activated because of a situation.

In the last two phases, the interest develops into a personal interest. Meaning that it is independent of any outside influence. The interest has become yours. You engage with the topic of interest because you desire to.

Phase 1

The first phase of interest development says that there is an external trigger that stimulates novelty or even cognitive dissonance. These triggers are very similar to what I mentioned earlier in the book. Such triggers will change the way you think and feel about a situation. The change in thought is what creates your "interest." Let me paint a picture of what this phase looks like for you.

Four characteristics will come with this phase of interest. First, attention will be present, but it will be very fleeting in nature. Second, the interest is highly dependent on external factors. By external factors, I mean a conversation, mentor, software, teacher, associate, pain, or any other form of stimuli. Third, the interest generated inside of you can be accompanied by positive or negative feelings. At this stage of interest, it doesn't have to create a positive emotion within. However, Renninger stresses the importance of positive affect for the *continued* development of interest to occur. Translation: if the interest produces negative feelings inside your heart, the interest won't make it to the next phase. Lastly, the interest is so low that it may or may not even be noticed.

Phase 2

In the second phase of interest development, the interest in the situation becomes maintained. When you reach the second stage, your willingness to continue with the interest after an external stimulus has triggered you is apparent.

At this point, a support system will emerge to help you find the ties between the interest and the unique traits you can bring to it. You will start identifying what you are good at within the interest. The development of knowledge, a sense of the content's value, and positive feelings around the interest are also introduced.

Phase 3

When the third phase comes around, things start to make a significant shift. At this point, you are more likely to engage with the interest on your own. You no longer need any external source to motivate you to act. Curiosity also peeks its head into the picture. Questions arise around the interest that inspires you to investigate and seek new information.

The positive feelings and the knowledge around the interest also take on new heights. The foundations and fundamentals begin to take root in your mind. However, you aren't satisfied with *only* knowing the basics. Your curiosity pushes you to dive deeper into the interest. Your sense of value for the content begins to shift to the laws and principles around the interest.

The Final Phase

In the fourth phase, the interest is now a well-developed personal interest. You _will_ engage with the interest on your own. Two noteworthy differences exist when an interest is fully developed.

First is the willingness to seek personal growth. Constructive feedback is searched for in efforts to evolve within the discipline. Another addition is perseverance. At this level of interest, your will is so strong that you develop the ability to persevere through frustrations to meet a goal. There is also an awareness of what others have contributed to the discipline. There is admiration and respect for what *the greats* have attributed within the discipline. In addition, there is a personal level of accountability to refine questions and seek answers. These traits contribute to sustained growth within the interest.

The second difference is the adaptation of principles and values. With this level of interest, you are so vested that you are willing to adopt the laws of success within the interest into your spirit. This is when people are willing to *become* composers, messengers, saviors, leaders, liberators, Imagineers, pioneers, or any other interests. Personal principles, beliefs, and values will be adjusted to those widely accepted within the discipline. This is where passions live.

Renninger and Hidi's interest model was developed primarily for academia. However, I believe the concept of interest within this model can be widely applied to any area of life. In this case, it is a great model for discovering and developing passions.

Certain qualities of the fourth phase, well-developed individual interest, are staples of a passion. These staples are perseverance, sought-after constructive criticism, self-initiated engagement, recognition of high-level performers, ownership of seeking answers to complex questions, and the adaptation of The Big 3: Principles, Values, and Beliefs. *When your interests take on these qualities, they have transformed into passions.*

Revealing Your Expertise

Regarding having expertise, there are varying elements of the equation. With passions, we discussed how our interests develop over time and eventually become passions. With your expertise, your wisdom, or skills, come from the reception and absorption of Truth. Notice I used three different terms: Expertise, Wisdom, and Skill. All three can be used interchangeably.

Wisdom is more valuable than all our precious stones here on Earth. Nothing that you desire can compare to its immense value. But what is wisdom? Wisdom is the ability to repeatedly implement Truth to receive a favorable and predictable result. This is a skill! When you can execute at this level, you become an expert. If you need more clarity around what you are good at, look for the areas in life where you can repeatedly apply a Truth and receive a favorable and predictable result.

Just as different interest levels lead to passion, there are different phases that lead to expertise. At the lowest level, you have a knowledge of Truth. It just means that you are aware of the Truth's existence. This means that you know what works.

Let's use a cell phone, for example. Nearly everyone has a cell phone nowadays. Are you an expert with your cell phone? Probably *not*. You probably just *know* how to use it. You may even be pretty good at using it. When you have knowledge of Truth, you can *know* how to use it, but not how to get a favorable and predictable result.

The second level is when you understand the principles behind the Truth. You know why and how it works when you fully receive the Truth. With this level of understanding, you can troubleshoot and solve problems. What if you *understood* the Truth about how and why your cell phone worked? The charging connection could break on your phone, and you could fix it. Or, if your screen went out, you could diagnose and discover the problem.

When you gain wisdom, your accumulated understanding and knowledge allow you to produce favorable and predictable results. You'll even be able to do so under adverse circumstances. That's why when something happens with your phone, who do you go see...probably an expert! The only way to become an expert is through repeated application.

When you repeatedly practice anything understood, it will begin to become *automatic*. This is wisdom.

There is a caveat with this as well. Within each skill, you may not be an expert in totality. Still, you may have mastered different disciplines within that topic. Continuing with the cell phone example, you may be an expert within a niche. For example, you may be no expert with the cell phone as a whole, but you may be an expert user (even though you are no expert at repairs). Be sure to examine different disciplines, or niches, within a subject to check for expertise.

But what does this information have to do with your dharma? To find out your unique skills, you only have to make a list of the things you know about. Make as long of a list as you can. Don't leave anything out. Be sure to write even the most trivial things you can think of alongside the most noteworthy things that come to mind.

Then, make another list next to it. In the second list, take a long, hard look at the list of things you know and find out which things you understand. Don't be shy about this list, either! Write everything down. Next to the list of understanding, you will write out a list of wisdom! Which of the things on your list of understanding can you use to repeatedly create a favorable and predictable result despite underlying circumstances?

The Emotion Attractor

Another great way to find what you are skilled at is to think about what you do to bring joy to others. It could be the smallest thing you do that makes someone else laugh, feel inspired, confident, encouraged, or capable.

Think about the times you remember bringing someone else to tears of joy. Is there something you've done on multiple occasions to bring heightened positive emotions to someone else? Whatever that thing is for you, it could be a gift you are blessed with.

Another way of finding what you're great at is to look at what you create. Do you create within the tangible realm or the intangible realm? Some people naturally gravitate to and are great at using their hands to create. And they do create spectacular things within the material world. Others create within the intangible realm. They create things like laughter, enthusiasm, curiosity, or joy. These answers can help you point to the things that you excel at.

Compassion – Unveiling the Needs of the World

There are many things that the world needs to retain order. No person alone can perform all the good works needed for the world to function. Also, everyone won't be inspired to do the same things. That's why everyone's dharma is connected to other people through service.

Your service is connected to the order needed in the world that calls to your heart. Some things need to be restored to their natural order. Others need upkeep to retain natural order. Lastly, other forms of order are yet to be revealed.

What about the order in the world stirs up emotion inside of you? Harriet Tubman chose to restore order in several people's lives, even at the risk of her own. She was driven to bring human relations back to its natural order.

What act of violence, waste, misuse, or abuse could you talk about for hours at a time? What injustices, gaps, wrongs, changes, additions, areas of potential, and/or possibilities catch your eye in the world? What gets you fired up within your culture and makes your skin crawl with disgust?

If nothing comes to mind, maybe you were meant to reveal order. Similar to the Wright Brothers, who showed the world that we are capable of defying the law of gravity by using the law of lift. What endeavor consumes your thoughts but has yet to be shown to the world? Is there something you *wholeheartedly* believe is possible, even though everyone else says it can't become a reality?

Still, retaining order could be what's calling you. Maybe you've had an experience as a child that you want to pass on to others. Everyone has something that grabs their attention and sparks their emotions. There is something in the world that grabs your mind every time it meets one of your senses.

These things may go unnoticed by you. They are so ingrained into you that your zeal and passion for the needs in the world may seem normal to you. You may think, "Doesn't everyone feel the same way about this"? Realistically, everyone doesn't view it with the same energy and emotion as you. However, it may have never crossed your mind that nobody else has the same eagerness as you! These are the things in your heart you need to go fishing for.

Your Network of Connectivity

The needs of the world are something that many people don't consider. To assist you in revealing the compassions that have been planted in your heart, here are two questions to help open your mind: 1) What does your personal world need 2) What does our global world need?

Your personal world consists of your associates, close friends, family, co-workers, etc. It's basically your network. We are all connected to a vast network of people. This network makes and shapes your "personal" world. No matter how big or small your personal world may be, think of the people in it and what they need.

What would make your personal world a better place? Are there problems that exist? What is missing? Have you heard anybody voice their opinion about what needs to be improved or eliminated? What are some solutions that will solve these problems? What are the services, products, knowledge, facilities, or resources that will elevate your personal world? The things that catch your eye may be the very calling you've been searching for.

The global world consists of the entire planet outside of your personal world. The issues within your personal world are one thing, but outside of that lies an entirely different set of problems waiting to be solved. Apply the same questions from the last paragraph and answer them in correlation with the global world.

Do the issues in your world also apply to the global world? If so, these may be some things you want to pay special attention to. Since you have a personal link to these issues, you have unique insights that others may not be aware of. Your personal experience gives you the ability to create solutions that others cannot.

You must focus on the solutions and not the problems. Ask yourself the questions so you can identify what the problems are. But your focus should be on creatively coming up with solutions. The solutions are what the world needs.

Finding Your Connections

One thing that will help will be to consider who will be impacted if you don't accomplish your purpose or fulfill your work. I once heard a man say, "One man's obedience is tied to so many other people's destiny."

Consider for just one moment all of the lives that your life is connected to. And then think about all the lives that their lives are connected to. Also, all of the lives that those people are connected to. It's all one *massive* network. And you're the central piece at the hub.

Your network is bigger than you believe it to be. Your life touches more lives than you think. When you execute and live to your fullest potential, it would be hard to fathom the positive impact you would have on an infinite number of people. This is the power of your reach when you provide value to the world through the unique order you offer.

In contrast, if you don't use your resources to cultivate your life's purpose, you have the exact same impact but in a neutral or negative way. In this sense, there are tons of individuals whose success depends on you! Accept the responsibility and the task of pushing yourself beyond what you believe to be your limits, not only for you but even more so for the people you are connected to.

The Tools of Revelation

Have you ever met yourself? One lovely evening, you get dressed in your best clothes for a charity event downtown. To add a bit of mystery and excitement to the event, it has been themed as a *masquerade* party. As you arrive, you notice that the masks others are wearing are very lavish. It's hard to tell who anyone is behind their mask.

As you begin to mingle, you notice someone you know just as they have lowered their mask for a brief moment. You make your way over to them to pay your respects. As the two of you are speaking, a third individual makes their way over to the two of you. After a brief introduction, your acquaintance steps away, leaving you with a stranger.

Reluctantly, the two of you begin to get to know one another. The more you learn about this person, the more intrigued you become. Without your awareness, two hours of conversation with this intriguing stranger has slipped by, and the party is nearly over.

The host steps in front of the microphone and, before bidding everyone farewell, instructs all the guests to take off their masks. You and your new associate lower your masks at the same time. With a confused gaze, you look at a mirror image of yourself.

Without your knowledge, you had been spending the entire night meeting yourself.

The average person has yet to decide what they want out of life. They've never seriously considered what type of person they need to be with, the best place to live, how they can add value to the world, how they want to be remembered, and many other things. If you feel like this, it may be because you are not tuned into "you."

Considering the state of the world, this is not surprising. We wake up first thing in the morning and reach for our phones. We get to work and spend the entire day solving problems on another person or company's behalf. Then we come home hoping to unwind enough so we have enough energy to do it all over again tomorrow (this is a perfect example of someone whose dimensions of purpose are too small).

When this happens, we never have time to think about what we want from life. There's certainly no time or energy to pursue these things, even if you become aware of them. Instead, there is just enough time to sit around and do *nothing. Spending* all your free time doing things that help you escape the reality of your life doesn't help you find out who you have become, not to mention who you are intended to be.

As a result, you have yet to decide what you want to do, who you should be, where you want to be, and who you should be around. The answer is simple in theory but difficult in practice. Simply, you need to spend some time with yourself. Free from all electronics, wi-fi, and anything similar.

Bill Gates does this for 7-day periods two times a year. He stays thoroughly disconnected from the world. He refers to these 7-day periods as his "*think weeks.*" We all need something similar to this. The time you carve out for yourself should be spent indulging in what I call The Tools of Revelation: Prayer, Meditation, and Journaling.

These three tools are an invitation from your *true Self*. If you accept the invitation, over time, you will experience something similar to the story I just shared with you about the masquerade event. Prayer, journaling, and meditating will introduce you to yourself.

For anyone with trouble knowing themselves, you should consistently use these tools to chip away at the stone of your identity. Right now, you see a solid block of stone, but these three tools are like those of a stonecutter. If you do the work, all the details about who you are and who you are meant to become will eventually be revealed.

Journaling

Journaling has completely changed my life and helped me understand myself. It will do the same for you. The method I use for journaling is simple and effective when employed persistently. Here are the items I include in my personal journal: New Ideas, Gratitude, Affirmations, Prayer List, and Streams of Consciousness.

New Ideas are just what the name implies...new ideas. We often have ideas handed to us by God, and we lose them because we don't write them down. The shortest pencil (or keystroke) is longer than the longest memory. I write down any ideas that have come to my mind that day: inventions, business ideas, parenting tips, relationship advice, money plans, book ideas, content, prayers, etc. If a thought comes to me early or mid-day, I immediately make a note on my phone and pull it back out during my journaling time. This isn't a practice that is meant to be analyzed and scrutinized. I write down *all my* ideas, whether they seem good or bad. Stay away from labeling your ideas. Just get them out of your head. You'd be surprised how many ideas you'll accumulate over time.

Gratitude is a practice that is sworn by all the greats. It is a great way to stay detached from the future and the past. Studies show that gratitude can have a positive effect on self-esteem, depression, emotions, resilience, anxiety, stress, decision-making, sleep, and even recovery from coronary-related conditions1. What a list!

I usually write 5 things I am grateful for: 1) something or someone from my past, 2) something or someone in my life right now, 3) the accomplishment of a goal that has yet to happen, 4) something in nature, and 5) something seemingly insignificant.

Affirmations are great little tools to keep you going. Jim Rohn used to say, "What follows the I am will always come looking for you." Solomon, one of the wisest men to ever walk the Earth, says that the tongue holds the power of life and death. If you could play a tape of all the words that follow your I am statements, I bet you'd be surprised.

After doing my affirmations for some time, I've become meticulously aware of what follows my personal "I am" statements and others around me. In your journal, write down 5 I am statements that will serve you. They don't have to be the same every day. But if you have 5 that you'd love to focus on, that's even better.

Prayer Lists are another great tool that keeps me centered. My prayer list usually stays the same, with a few adjustments here and there. This is important to me because it's hard for me to remember everything I need to pray about. I know nothing has been left out when I have a list, and it serves as a constant reminder. It also helps you to be more aware when your prayers are brought to fruition.

Streams of Consciousness is a shorter version of Julia Cameron's Morning Pages. Julia suggests that many blocked artists can benefit from writing their consciousness onto a page. There is only one rule. Write down any and everything that comes into your mind. Once the pen strokes or the keyboard taps, you can't stop until three pages are full. It can be gibberish, anger, or even something that makes you cry. It doesn't matter what comes out. Just be sure to write down whatever comes into your mind.

I like to use what happened during my day as a prompt. Also, I usually fill a minimum of one page. Sometimes, I can write for 5 pages, and on some days, it's only one page. The number of pages isn't the most significant thing. The most significant thing is getting as much as possible out of your mind.

Meditation

Many guided meditations are free and can help free your mind from unwanted thoughts. My favorite is simply sitting in a quiet space with an erect spine. And observe your breath. Focus on your breath as you inhale and exhale. As your focus shifts to your breath, your thoughts will begin to vanish. Periodically, your thoughts will come back. Just shift your focus back to your breath. Begin with smaller durations and gradually build up to longer durations.

Prayer

Praying is one of the most powerful things you can do for yourself. Especially praying out loud so that your ears can hear. Faith is produced in the ears. Faith is the most precious raw material on the face of the Earth. The fact that we can produce it by merely speaking is information that can change your life if you're willing to use it. If you don't believe in prayer, then leave it out.

If you don't believe, but you are open to doing it, give it a try. Use a model prayer if you have no clue what to pray about. You could also make a list of things you'd like to get rid of and things you'd like to gain in your life. Praying about the things on that list could be a great place to start.

If you do these three things, an event will eventually occur. I call this event *meeting yourself.* It will take time, patience, and persistence, but you will be introduced to who you are if you do not give up. A word of caution. The more you get to know yourself, you may not like what you find.

I've found that self-awareness can sometimes be a double-edged sword. Awareness can create one of two things. It can create movement toward a solution, or it can paralyze you. For example, let's say you've lived in a house for ten years with no problems. But one day, you accidentally put a giant hole through the drywall when hanging a picture. After doing so, you realize (become aware) that there are 1000s of roaches inside the walls.

You have now become aware of the problem. You can become so paralyzed by fear and disgust that you no longer desire to live in the house. Or the situation can move you toward a solution to a problem you were blind to.

Could you imagine what you'd do with yourself for a week being entirely disconnected from the world? You could even throw fasting in there for a day or more if you feel up to the challenge. Go out in nature and just observe your surroundings. These are all great ways to spend time with yourself and get in tune with who you are.

This could be precisely what you need to reveal your passions, compassion, and expertise. This may sound like insanity. But the true definition of insanity is continuing with the same pattern and expecting something different to arise. If you want a change in your life, you must be courageous enough to try something different.

The Rendezvous

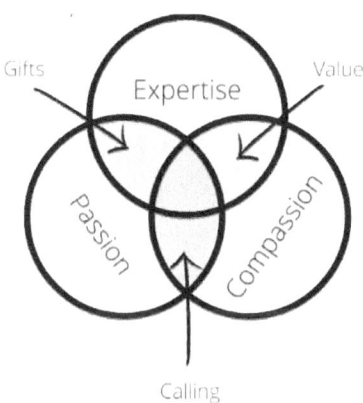

Once you have clarity on the three components of your dharma, you can dig even deeper and reveal more about yourself. Where the components overlap, you will discover more of your unique traits. The additional areas of revelation are your gifts, value, and calling. Where your passions and your expertise meet, you will find your gifts. Expertise and compassion converge to reveal your value. Lastly, your passion and compassion come together to raise the volume of your calling. We'll begin by discussing how your gifts will appear within this model.

Opening Your Gifts

Another item that everyone has is a gift. Everyone has been given a unique gift that fits perfectly into their dharma, their true nature. Many people have multiple gifts, even though they may not be aware of them. After reading the scripture, "Your gift shall make room for you," I was on the hunt to reveal what felt like a mystery in my life.

Trying to find someone who could point me in the right direction, I would ask everyone around me if they knew what their gift was. I even asked a few people what they thought my gift was. None of that helped much. The only thing that helped was two-fold. First, I had to get to know myself better through The Tools of Revelation. Second, I had to search within.

But what are gifts in the first place? There's a reason that I explained the three ingredients for dharma. They not only reveal your dharma, but they also reveal other aspects of your dharma. Through the process of unveiling your dharma, you will be brought to your gifts. Your gifts are located at the place where your passions and your expertise meet.

If you thoroughly understand what passions and expertise are, then you can do the work to reveal your own. As you reveal these two, items will crossover between them. These items that show up as a passion and expertise are your gifts. Please read that again. That statement alone can shave years off of your search.

Your gift is the key that unlocks your future. The gift activates the value that you have to offer the world. It is the tool that opens up your "space." Just as you use a key to unlock a door, you also use your gift to unlock your future. Exceeded in value by only a few rare items, your gift is nearly as precious a gem as wisdom. Do not take this lightly.

If you placed as much faith into your gift as you do your career, education, money, and many other fleeting desires of this world, you'd exceed all of what you perceive to be your limitations. The answer you've been searching for, and the solution you've been trying to create is inside your gift. Your gift comes to you as naturally as your breathing. Let that ruminate in your mind. Well-developed personal interest and wisdom combine to create your gift. Both of which come to you naturally.

Why are we given gifts? The Creator gave us gifts for energy and service. When you use your gifts, you can replenish energy at an equal to or higher rate than you relinquish energy. As you use energy, it is given back to you. What if for every dollar you spent on your gifts, you received $2 back. You'd spend every dollar you had as fast as you could.

This is how our gifts work with our energy. The other reason for our gifts is for servitude. We were given gifts to give them freely to others *for their benefit*. Our gifts are used as a tool to serve others. Your gift is a tool to solve the world's problems. This means that we must utilize our gifts to aid us in fulfilling one or even all of the purposes for humanity: 1) Retaining order, 2) Restoring order, and 3) Revealing order.

Finding Your Value

The late Myles Munroe used to say that if you want to succeed, you only need to become a person of value. There is a unique value that you and only you can add to the world. Just consider the people that are of great value to our lives. They hold great significance. The impact and effect they have upon the very fiber of our beings are paramount. Have you ever considered the magnitude of the value that exists within you?

Value is usually placed upon an item because of its rarity. Things that are easily accessible and high in quantity are of the least value. This is why it is so significant that you *be yourself*. Why? Because there is nobody else on planet Earth that can be you as good as you can.

When you discover the unique value you can provide to the world, you must step into it as *yourself*. The *you* that God intended you to become, not the *you* that your world has molded. When you step into your value as your *true* Self, people will flock to you because of the *rare* nature of what you give.

Your value is found where your expertise and compassion overlap. You have stepped into your value when you reveal a genuine need in the world that aligns with your natural wisdom. This is the service you are obligated to provide to the world. These are the areas of life you're intended to have dominion over.

Answering the Call

My dad often had me answer his phone when I was little. When I'd pick it up, he'd look at me and whisper, "I am not here!" He was *always* helping other people out. So, when he had a moment to himself, he did not want to be bothered by anybody.

I am sure you have had a moment like this as well. Somebody calls you, and when you pick it up and see who it is on the other end, you put the phone back down. You could be busy doing something else. Or, you may not be interested in talking to that person. You may know they only call to ask for something, and you have nothing to give. Whatever the reason, you're not *interested* in picking up that phone.

Do you remember the magic word for discovering your passions: *interest!*? Your passion is the first component of the call that comes from your purpose. You will have a *well-developed individual interest* in picking up that call.

The funny thing about a call is that someone is always on the other end. The calling you feel compelled to answer will always be tied to other people. That is the second part of the call: *compassion*. There will be a direct connection to the people you are supposed to serve.

The only thing is that there will always be other calls. The call from your dharma will be one of many calls you will receive. Many things in life will pull at your heartstrings. The other calls are attractive but can be deceptive. Similar to the cell phone you own, there isn't just one person that can contact you.

In addition, the call from your dharma will be full of uncertainty and fear. You may want to answer it, but you don't know if you can deliver for the person on the other end. You probably aren't confident that you can come through for them. *That call* is the one you absolutely need to pick up!

The good thing is the call will never stop ringing until you answer it. The ring may sometimes fade away because of the noise in the world. But it will never stop. You will always feel an empty spot in your heart until you pick up that phone and serve your people.

You have a calling. It sits at the meeting place of your passions and compassions. There will be apparent similarities between what you are passionate about and the order needed in the world. It may be presented in general terms, but that is okay. The specifics will be ironed out along the way. You just have to be willing to answer the call.

Essence & Form

A quick word about the essence and the form of your dharma. It is important that you only cling to and *primarily* be concerned with the essence of your dharma. That is the identity that your dharma reveals. Who do you need to become to embody your dharma? What beliefs do you need to internalize? What beliefs do you need to let go of? This is the essence of your dharma.

Many people are attached to the form their dharma takes. The form that your dharma presents itself with is often where we receive meaning. Your purpose is attached to your dharma's essence. Your dharma may take on many forms throughout your life. Some will hurt as they leave and transition into a different form.

Whereas your form will go through seasons of change and seasons of being static. Your essence is like liquid. It has the capacity to take on any form. No matter what form is present, *your true Self* will also be there.

For example, after reading this book, you will have discovered your dharma, purpose, or true nature. When you fully embrace your dharma, it will reveal itself even before your vision has come to fruition.

Here is another example. What would happen if I were to take an Olympic runner and switch minds with someone out of shape? The essence of the Olympic runner would present itself in the body of the out-of-shape person, even though his/her Olympic frame is not there.

The same is true in the reverse; the essence of the out-of-shape person would present itself even in the body of the Olympic runner. It won't happen immediately, but their essence will manifest in physical reality. This means the Olympic runner who was placed into the form of an out-of-shape person will eventually take on the form of an Olympic runner. And the out-of-shape person placed into the form of the Olympic runner will eventually become out of shape.

This is why embodying the essence of your dharma is far more critical than the current form in your life. The essence will remain no matter what happens in life. It will always be there after a loved one passes, after a career move, after an ailment, or any other form-altering change. You mustn't attach to form because your form will change, but your true nature is eternal.

The Law of Impermanence exists within the realm of time. This law says that *everything* that lives in time changes. Nothing stays the same. However, your dharma does not live in time. As I have said, your purpose was created before your physical body. It can continue after your physical body is no more.

Since your dharma does not abide by the laws of time, it does not change. But all six things we have discussed so far (passion, compassion, expertise, gifts, value, and calling) are forms that your dharma manifests through.

These forms of your dharma live in time. Because they live in time, they *have to* abide by the law of impermanence. They can change and often do. For this reason, you must focus more on your dharma than the forms it manifests through. The forms of your dharma are remarkable blessings and deserve much attention. But they should not be prioritized over the essence of your eternal nature. Remember that these six vital qualities of your uniqueness come from your dharma, not the other way around.

Revealing Your Dharma – Peeling Back The Layers

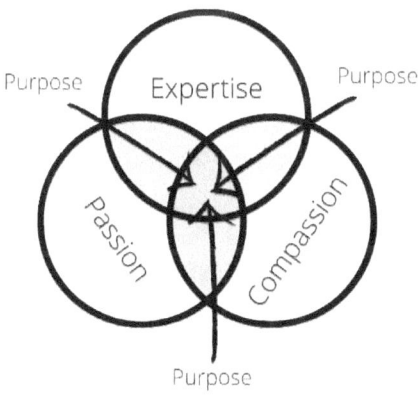

Now is the time to put everything together. I've thoroughly explained all the components connected to your dharma: Passions, Compassion, Skills, Gifts, Value, and Calling. These are like directional arrows pointing to your life's purpose. As you go through the exercise, keep that thought in mind. This process is simple but powerful.

Part 1 – The First Layer

The first layer of the process requires you to find anything you have available to document your thoughts. This can be a piece of paper, a whiteboard, a computer, or anything else. Whatever you feel most comfortable using. You will make three columns to reveal the first layer and label each with passion, compassion, and expertise.

Start with one column until you've listed as many things as possible that come to mind. Don't hesitate to list even the most minor things you can think of. If you can get to 100 items, then do so. After you've completed one column, I've found it helpful to cover the completed list so you cannot see it. Once the second column is complete, cover it up before moving on to the final column.

If you are having trouble listing items, go back and re-read the corresponding section. This will help you think of items you may not have at the top of your mind. Also, time is your friend here, not your enemy. Sometimes, it may be helpful to re-read the corresponding section above and then walk away from the list for a while. Let your mind do its magic.

Refrain from going into any activities that you feel compelled to engage in as a form of escapism. You may feel frustrated and uneasy as you list these things. It is important not to force it in this case. Instead, leave the list as it is. Persistently continue with the three tools of revelation and revisit the list after a few weeks or even a few months. You may need more time with yourself for the deeper truths about yourself to come out.

If you choose to do this exercise with someone else, do so with someone you trust. Your partner needs to be someone you feel comfortable opening up and being vulnerable with. Leaving them out of this process is best if they make you uncomfortable.

Part 2 – The Second Layer

The second part of this process is to search for similarities. You must have used the tools of revelation for an adequate amount of time. The tools will give you a deep understanding of who you really are. This ensures there is nothing in your first layer that is *artificial*. In other words, anything that isn't truly of you but instead of the many influences of your world.

These things will present within the first layer as anything that stems from fear and/or immoral activity. The tools of revelation will reveal to you why things of this nature have been an attachment and allow you to release from them. Also, they will allow you to meet yourself. Meeting yourself ensures that nothing that is a part of who you truly are is left out in the first layer.

You will now begin your search for overlapping qualities. Remember that these overlapping spaces represent your gifts, value, and calling. This will be like a word search. You are looking for words that appear in two different columns.

As you find them, circle them. If you don't see any identical words, look for synonyms. If you still can't find any, start looking for words that are complementary and/or correlated to one another. As a label, write beside the pair of words a g, v, or c for gifts, value, and calling, respectively. Your findings represent these three.

You may find that you have many gifts, multiple callings, or different areas of value. This is a good thing. If you find multiples, this is what I want you to do. Find the gift that scares you the most, the value you think no one could use, and the calling you feel you aren't worthy of answering. Place the number one beside these items after you've located them.

Your enemy often places fear directly in front of the things you will be best at. Everything you are destined for is on the other side of that fear. The other things that present themselves as one of the three may be used as support for your main thing. The others could point to the uniqueness you're destined to bring to that gift, calling, or value.

Having multiple in an area could also point to your rarity. You may be predestined to use these things in conjunction with one another. It may be a combination that no one else has done. Or it could be a combination that no one could do like you.

If you have a ton of similarities, look for the words within each column that are similar. For example, look for all the words in the passion column that are similar in nature. Find the synonyms. Locate the pairs. Connect the words or phrases in that column from the same root. Find as many of them as you can. Take similar words from that column and transform them into one word that embodies them all. Then, do the same for the other two columns as well.

Part 3 – Your Dharma

The last part is revealing your dharma. When you come to this point, you are now looking for the word (or words) that appears in all three columns. When I did this exercise for the second time, I only found one word that fit into all three. You may have to look for synonyms to find one that appears in all three. There may be a third word that means the same as the other two, which may require some digging.

Once you've found it, I want you to make a word tree. Take out another sheet of paper and put the word found in all three columns in the center of the paper. Circle the word. Write out another word that represents that word anywhere on the sheet of paper. Don't overthink this. Circle that word as well. Then, draw a line between the two words. Repeat this process using as many words as you can. If you get stuck, use a thesaurus to find more words. Be sure to only use the words that you feel a connection to.

After completing the process, you will find that all the words on the paper fully represent the activities you naturally gravitate to. The things that people think of when they hear your name. Activities that you are naturally good at. People come to you for help in these areas.

All of the words are a part of your true nature. The word at the center is a representation of all of these things. The word at the center is who you are intended to be. It is the essence of who you are in your spirit. When I first did this, I was amazed at the words I was connected to. I had been doing these things all my life, yet I was oblivious to them.

Recall what I said about all the greats who came before us.

All of the greatest people who have been revered for centuries, or even millennia in some cases, all focused on their being. Moses was born to be a Leader. Paul of Tarsus was born to be a messenger. Abraham was born to be a father. Jesus was born to be a savior. Gandhi, MLK, and Mandela were born to be liberators. Michelangelo was born to be an artist. Isaac Newton was born to be an observer. Thomas Edison and The Wright Brothers were born to be inventors. Beethoven and Mozart were born to be composers. William Shakespeare was born to be a writer. Socrates was born to be a thinker. Walt Disney was born to be an Imagineer."

This word is a representation of who *you* were born to *be*! It is your true nature. A mirror of your eternal Self. All the words you wrote are smaller pieces that make up the whole. Remember, all the pieces that point to your dharma are like directional arrows. Your dharma is the main piece of the puzzle that makes you who you are.

You can see your vision now that you know who you are meant to be. When you see your vision, you can better understand what you are supposed to do. I understand that knowing what you are supposed to be doing is a topic of interest for nearly everyone.

We will discuss these things in a later chapter. Just remember what I spoke of earlier about essence and form. What you have just revealed is the essence of your dharma. What you are supposed to do in life is the form your dharma will manifest as in this world.

Coach's Challenge: The first time I did this exercise, it didn't end well. I finished, and I was a little confused. Instead of feeling empowered, I felt defeated. I had recently started journaling but hadn't been doing it too long. I let about 6 months go by of journaling and self-reflecting. I did this exercise again, and it had a completely different outcome. There wasn't a drastic change in who I was, but I walked away with a stronger understanding of my purpose. I did it a 3rd time about 6 months later, and my understanding grew again.

It's like re-reading a book. The first time you read it is good. When you re-read it, you realize there were gaps in your understanding. There are parts of the book you don't even remember that stick out the second go around. If you read it a third time, it's an even more powerful experience. The impression the material has on you takes a different form. Yet, you may still see aspects of the book from a different perspective because of your evolved understanding.

This is how it is with this exercise. Because of this, I challenge you to do the same as I did. Don't do this once just to check the box as complete. Make this a regular occurrence alongside consistent use of the Tools of Revelation. Like a good book, come back and revisit this exercise every 4-6 months and watch how your understanding of your purpose blossoms!

This exercise has a very spiritual nature to it. It will require you to have a strong awareness of who you are. If you haven't taken me up on any of these challenges up to this point, I strongly suggest that you do this one.

Archetypes

To provide more guidance and direction, many dharma teachings include some form of a series of archetypes. This is to help categorize the many different types of natural personalities to make it easier to pinpoint your unique combination. I didn't mention these for a specific reason.

There may be a word or phrase that describes your unique nature that only you know and understand. A particular combination of words may be revealed to you by The Creator as you go through the exercises that I could never express to you. I have provided a framework that puts you in a headspace that opens your mind so you can be receptive to what naturally flows.

There is nothing wrong with archetypes, assessments, and the like. They serve their purpose. For this framework, I want you to listen until your ears are open enough to hear the answers you seek.

When I first went through the exercises with my wife and daughter, they looked at me and said, "What's next?" I had no clue! I looked at everything on my paper and couldn't find an answer. It wasn't until I consistently did my journal work that my eyes opened. I had to learn more about myself to have more thoughts, ideas, and personal revelations to work with. I went through the process again about 7 months later, and it was as if my dharma pulled out a megaphone and screamed it through the paper.

So, you may find yourself going through the exercise and finding that nothing aligns. You may discover that nothing has overlaps to reveal your gifts, calling, and value. That is okay. If this happens, I have two suggestions for you.

First, start or keep going with the three tools of revelation: Prayer, Journaling, and Meditation. The more I used the tools, the more I revealed about myself. Something would happen during the day, and I'd become anxious to write about it. I knew I had to write it down before it escaped my mind. Little revelations and answers would appear from a conversation, a book I had read before, a thought or image in my mind, or sometimes just from a shower.

When these things happen, don't hesitate to beeline to your journal and write it down before it escapes you. You can easily take out your phone and make a voice note if your journal is not around. I love doing this. Find a way to record yourself talking and speak from the heart about your ideas, thoughts, and feelings. You could also use whatever resources are available to trap the thought before it escapes your mind. Use a piece of paper, send yourself an email, or just use your phone. Do whatever you must to get the thought out of your mind. You can then add it to your journal later.

The *second* suggestion is to let the tools of revelation do their thing. Give it some time and return to the exercise after a few months and see how many things have made their way into your mind. Also, be sure to review your journal every few weeks or so to read what you've written. This is often where the magic happens.

I don't know about you, but I can barely remember what I did a week ago. With the tens of thousands of thoughts running through my mind every day, it is easy for things to get lost. Going through the journal to read your thoughts from the past is revealing. As you go through this process and return to the exercise, you'll also find that it will be like someone turned on the light for you. You will meet yourself within the pages of your journal. You will uncover your interests, desires, beliefs, limitations, etc.

So again, the archetypes that tell you what you like and don't like and your unique personality are outstanding. However, trust me when I say that using this process is spiritual and will serve you. It may take a little more time, but however long it takes, it will undoubtedly beat the 30-40 years that statistics reveal it takes the average person. Remember, persistently stick to the tools and employ patience; your dharma will reveal itself.

A Call for Courage

Bronnie Ware worked as a palliative nurse who stayed with and cared for individuals in the last 12 weeks of their life. She worked this job for eight years. One could only imagine the amount of death Bronnie had to experience. The conversations she was a part of must have had to be second to none. Some of the conversations were so sparking that she wrote a blog post titled "Inspirations and Choi," which became so popular that she turned it into a book.

In her book, she wrote about the top 5 regrets she found among those she cared for as they endured their last days. I find it to be quite the debacle that the biggest regret from individuals staring death in the face was not having the courage to live the life they felt they could have lived.

Knowing your dharma is one thing. But having the courage to step into it, with all its uncertainty, is another issue. This is why it is essential to be willing to do the work of emptying yourself of your fear, doubt, and indecision-based programming. You could hear an audible voice from God himself telling you what to do, who to talk to, when to do it, and how to do it. However, if you are still controlled by the fears your limiting beliefs have placed within, you won't have the courage it takes to step into your dharma.

An important thing to note here is that fears are *not* dissipated. Fears are outgrown and conquered. I am a person who can consume a ton of information. I can watch eight hours of podcasts, sermons, and back-to-back seminars without missing a beat. One day, I watched a roundtable discussion with several noteworthy actors and directors.

One of the directors begins to tell a story about one of the movies he directed. He says they started shooting, and everything was going well. He continued his story by explaining that there is a point in every movie that is considered the *big scene*. This one scene can make or break the movie. There could be millions of dollars that go into this one scene. It has to go right because you can only blow up a car once, right!

To add to the pressure, thousands of people on set are waiting for your direction. When the day came to shoot this big scene, this guy insisted on staying in his trailer and not directing the rest of the movie! Apparently, it took quite a convincing for a few hours to get him to come out of the trailer and sit in the director's seat.

He explained how overwhelmed he felt that all these people depended on him to make the right calls. Who was this mystery guy? It was none other than Denzel Washington! Now, if you're an avid movie watcher, you know how experienced and talented Denzel is in the movie industry. I was stunned when I sat there listening to him tell this story.

I thought, "It must've been because it was his first time!" Then, the interviewer, seemingly stunned as well, asked Denzel if he still felt like that. Denzel says it doesn't matter if he's acting or directing; he always feels like that for big scenes. To my amazement, all the other directors expressed feeling the same way.

I then watched a few other interviews where other notable actors and actresses expressed the _exact_ same sentiments. In my mind, you'd think after all those years of performing, his experience would eventually kill the fear and doubt. The Truth is that fear and doubt will always be there. They must be trampled over with courage. That's what courage really is! Courage is not the absence of fear and doubt. Courage is action despite fear and any of fear's constituents.

Courage has constituents, too. Self-confidence is one of them. Whenever those two get together, obstacles move out of the way, and possibilities open up. Your dharma can't be activated until you embrace a courageous attitude, even in the face of uncertainty and incapability. Don't be one of the gifted individuals who regret letting fear and its many associates prevent your dharma from being given to the world!

Chapter 6 Summary:

- In revealing your purpose, it is vital that you identify who you are at all three layers of Self: body, mind, and spirit. The more you tap into who you are, the easier it will be to see your purpose. This is so because of the essence of purpose. Purpose is not a task, goal, or a possession but a state of being.

- Your Dharma (eternal purpose) is the culmination of your compassion, passion, and expertise. When these three converge, your purpose makes an appearance.

- Journaling, meditation, and prayer make up The Tools of Revelation. These can be used as a mirror for your mind and spirit. Using them will help you get to know who you *actually* are. As a result of getting to know yourself, you can unveil your expertise, compassion, and passions... the *prerequisites* of your purpose. Once these three are discovered, you can also reveal your gift, calling, and unique value.

- Use the "Peeling Back the Layers" exercise to help you reveal your purpose. Don't become frustrated if you feel uncomfortable or fail to find the answers you seek. This is a spiritual exercise and requires a strong knowledge of Self.

- Revealing purpose is but the beginning of a journey. This is a journey that is challenging and requires transformation. The road must be faced with courage and tenacity. Stay the course and step into the divine you!

CHAPTER 7

THE BLUEPRINT:

How To Design The Blueprint For Living Out Your Life's Mission

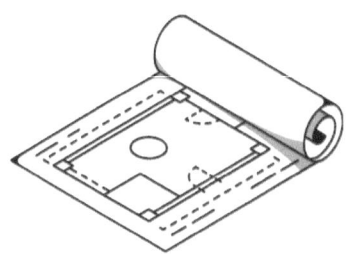

D o you remember that analogy I gave earlier about building a house and your life's purpose? "*When a house is built, different materials are used for the foundation, the home itself, and the furnishings inside the home. If you were a house, the foundation would be who you are (Purpose). The house itself would be what you do (Activity). The furnishing and décor would constitute what you have (Property). Your priority should always be on the foundation.*"

We've focused this entire book on understanding and revealing who you are and who you are destined to become. But what happens after you have revealed your *true* life's purpose? A home's foundation may not be the sexiest thing in the world, but it is the most significant.

Now that you have established a solid foundation, you can start designing the home. You have all the necessary tools and materials to design and build your *dream home*. This is the part of the book where you find out what you are supposed to be doing in your life.

As you go through the blueprint, remember what I mentioned earlier about the forms of your life's purpose (Passion, Compassion, Expertise, Value, Gift, Calling). They are like water. They hold the power to change their shape to fit many different roles, responsibilities, and relationships. While we hold the responsibility to plan, our steps are ordered by a Higher Power.

This is why the six forms of your life's purpose can change their shape. As a potter molds clay, they will be molded to ensure they bring your life's purpose to fruition. If you attach to a form, you will run the risk of removing its ability to shift its shape. If this happens, The Creator won't be able to adjust the form so that your life's purpose can be embodied. This isn't because He isn't *able*. *It* will be because you aren't willing.

The only exception is your mission. This mission will remain the same. Just as your life's purpose never changes, your mission won't change either. This is because there is a direct tie between your purpose and the mission. The mission will always be to become and remain in your life's purpose.

Since the purpose doesn't change, the mission won't change. Similar to your purpose, the component of your mission can also manifest in different forms in your life. The components of your mission are the vision and the plan. Just like the components of your dharma, these can change shape to account for life changes.

This ensures the mission can be accomplished through the adversity you will face. The six components of your life's purpose and the two components of your mission will work together to complete the mission. With these things in mind, we can start putting together the blueprint for your life.

Mission Possible - Finding Your People

At the time of this writing, I've been in the military for 7 years now. Every serviceman and woman knows it's all about the mission. Everything you do has to support the mission. Hundreds of jobs in the armed forces work together to support the mission.

People are sent on trips and training in support of the mission. There are smaller supportive missions within the grand scheme of the larger, more general mission. Trillions of dollars are spent to keep the mission going. Systems are set up to recruit new personnel consistently so the mission never dies.

The entire thing is one big mission, and everyone knows it. Leaders who command the troops imprint upon your heart the message of "mission first" from the time you enter the military ranks. This is why no matter what happens, you can always look at the person next to you and say, "It's all about the mission, right?" and they'll know exactly what you mean.

But what is a mission? A mission is a particular assignment given to an entity or an organization to possess dominion over. The organization that is your life has a mission as well. Although, your mission is much larger than anything the military has ever done.

The military has hundreds of thousands of people dedicated to serving the mission. Similarly, trillions of cells work within you to ensure the mission can progress. All of these cells strive to keep your resources alive and well. Every fiber of your being stands ready to be trained and put to work at your every command.

Without a mission, they retreat to their default setting: to keep you alive. But with a mission, they will work day and night to accomplish the objective. Many people go their entire lives without a mission. Their resources lie in default mode to keep their bodies alive while their spirit sits dormant, waiting for a mission to give them life.

Your mission will be a desire that stems from your purpose in life. When you delight in the things that are destined for you, specific desires will be given to you by the Creator. The desire will be to provide order for the world in one of order's three manifestations: Restoration, Retainment, or Revelation. This is the order that you are intended to bring to the world. This type of desire is insatiable. It will stay with you throughout your life, although it will manifest differently.

The Purpose Equation – Solving for Your People

The things in the world that you are supposed to fix are a direct result of your purpose. The mission directly reflects the uniqueness that makes you who you are. Let me explain. Four variables will always point directly to your purpose: Purpose, Production, The Problem, and The People.

These are the variables that help you solve the equation for purpose. Here is the equation: *The purpose for production always equals the inverse of the problem that your people have (P4P=1/P+P).* Here is a quick rundown of the variables of the equation.

You are the *production.* You were produced in the womb of your mother by God. Your parents were simply the vessels that The Creator used to get you here. Your production came with all your natural gifts, skills, etc.

Your *purpose* is the reason that you were created. This book has examined purpose in great detail.

The *problem* is the issue or suffering in the world that bothers you the most. It's the thing that your people suffer from the most. You will have a deep-seated desire that's been planted in your heart by the Creator to see this problem be solved. Whatever the problem may be in your heart, I can guarantee that you've noticed the problem several times throughout your life.

The "*people*" are the individuals you were predestined to serve your gifts to. The entire human race can benefit from your service. But there will always be a nation or tribe of people that you feel magnetized toward. These are the people that suffer from the problem that you're most drawn to. The half of this equation that includes your people is what constitutes your mission: *to serve your unique solution to your people.*

Your mission is generated when you find your people. If you've done the inner work I've suggested in this book, your people should be the only variable missing from the equation of purpose. If you don't know who your people are, look no further than within the problem in your world that's always bothered you. Take a deep look at your list of compassions. Who are the people that suffer most from that problem? The problem may affect everyone in the world, but who suffers *the most* from the problem?

The answer to that question points to your people. That answer will complete the equation. You are to use your identity to restore, retain, and/or reveal order within the problem that your people are suffering from. That problem is your intended area of dominion. That is your province.

Your mission is to produce a solution for that problem and serve it to your people. Make it accessible to all the people in that province.

Then, restore the problem to its natural order and control the order you've created.

Just as your purpose was within, so is your mission. You have to pull it out. The good news is that after doing so much inner work to reveal your purpose, the mission should be much simpler to piece together. Carrying out the mission will transform you into who you are meant to be. Your purpose is the intention of your production, but the mission is the tool of transformation.

Now that we have the last piece of the equation of purpose. We will put it all together in a life-purpose statement. It is a tool to help provide clarity. The one thing you will need before addressing your vision and your plan.

The Life Purpose Statement — Putting it All Together

> "A person without a purpose is like a ship without a rudder"
>
> – Earl Nightingale

Purpose-Spangled Banner

What's the one thing that rings true for every military installation? At 4:30, Monday through Friday, the national anthem plays. Loudspeakers are placed so the song can be heard anywhere on the base. If you are not inside a building, you are supposed to pay your respects to the national anthem.

If you are driving in a car, then you stop wherever you are and listen to the song. If you are outside a vehicle, you stop, stand at parade rest, and place your hand over your heart. For those in uniform, you pop to attention and salute toward the nearest flag.

Doesn't matter if you can't even see the flag. You face the nearest one you can recall seeing on the base and salute in that direction. For the roughly two minutes of that song, everything on the base is supposed to stop, and everyone listens and respects the flag.

Now, why would anybody institute such a mandate on a military institution? For one simple reason: to remember. To remember what? Purpose! The national anthem serves as a reminder of all the lives that fought for freedom. A reminder of the fallen and the wars of the past.

It's a reminder of *why* you serve. A reminder of why you are on the military base in the first place. It's easy to forget. The routine and seemingly urgent nature of everyday life can easily choke out the memory of why you do what you do.

A life purpose statement is to your life what the Star-Spangled Banner is supposed to be to military members. It's a reminder. A reminder of your life's purpose. So that you can stay on track. To keep the cares of life from choking out the very reason you were brought here. It's like an alarm clock intended to wake you up from the doldrums of routine and everyday life if needed. A slight nudge to the heart to keep you motivated.

Set a time to read your life purpose statement out loud every day. If you are uncomfortable doing this, make a voice note and listen to it. Just make sure that your ears can audibly hear the words. This do ye in remembrance of purpose! It wouldn't take but a few seconds of your day. The more times you read it per day, the better. But at the very minimum, it should be done at least once daily. Make the time sacred to you. Take a page from the military's book and stop whatever you are doing so you can *hear* your life's purpose. After all, it's only the purpose of *your* life.

The Compass

When was the last time you were lost? Do you remember what that felt like? Being lost is one of the worst feelings in the world. Having a life purpose statement is like having a compass. It's compact, simple, and reliable. Using your compass with a map (your vision and plan), you can prevent getting lost.

Ever had a big decision to make and weren't sure what you should do? Having a constant reminder of your life's purpose can help you stay on the *right* path. Pivotal decisions become effortless because the information about your life purpose is stored in your mind and will be heard daily.

When the data is readily available, it's easy to see if someone or something is taking you on a detour. The answer becomes evident if something or someone tries to enter your life and doesn't fit your life's purpose. Knowing which direction to avoid is just as important, if not more, as knowing where to go.

Writing Your Life Purpose Statement

A life purpose statement is a *concise* tool that sums up the meaning of your existence. It serves as a compass, a reminder, and answers the ultimate "why." It is a simplified visual representation of the equation for purpose: P4P = 1/P + P. It usually looks something like this:

*The Purpose for my life is to **be** a(n) _____ (your dharma) for _____ (your people)*

That's it! It's short, sweet, and straightforward. Nothing becomes dynamic until it becomes clear. In other words, your purpose will have *vitality* once it becomes crystal clear. Having clarity is like breathing the breath of life into your purpose. That's what simplicity does. As Goethe said, "Everything is both simpler than we can imagine and more complicated than we can conceive." Isaac Newton stated that "Nature is pleased with simplicity."

That one statement is simple. It's also very general. It's meant to be that way. *Remember, your purpose is not to be achieved. It is to be persistently personified.* It is manifested, not accomplished. Do not be alarmed by its simplicity. As Leonardo Da Vinci says, "Simplicity is the ultimate sophistication."

If you can manage to, try to be in a quiet place that is free from distractions. I also recommend that you pray before partaking in this activity.

If you've done everything I've mentioned up to this point, your foundation can't get any better. It is time to start designing the components of your mission.

Vision

When I was about 22, I occasionally taught bible class at church. I was so terrified of speaking in front of people that I would go over my lesson dozens of times until I got it like the back of my hand. At the time, I lived in an apartment complex.

One day, I took my daughter to the park inside that complex. As we were playing, I found myself standing on top of the jungle gym that was the peak of the playground. But as I turned around, my attention was immediately stolen by a field of corn (yes...a literal field of corn). I had never noticed the field before from ground level. But given a new perspective, it was the only thing I could see.

After that day, I started going to the top of that same jungle gym to go over my notes for my bible study lessons. That seemingly endless field of corn became my audience. After doing this for a few weeks, I began to see that seemingly endless *field of people* in my mind. I couldn't stop seeing it. I couldn't stop thinking about it.

I had no clue what it was supposed to mean. All I had was an intense belief that I would one day stand before these people as a beacon for change. No more and no less. Over time, it became clear that the field represented all the lives I was supposed to impact. It did not correlate with fame, money, or any other carnal desires.

My only desire was to impact others the same way that I was impacted by my mentors. I wanted to be a vessel and an example to the people in my vision. As I got older, the vision never escaped my imagination. Over time, it began to be choked out by the routine of everyday life and its responsibilities. But it gained a new light after some time. This time, I chose to give the vision precise details. It wasn't until I added the details that it sprouted into my life.

Just as your mission springs from your purpose, so does your vision spring from your mission. Your vision is a snapshot of your purpose. It is a clip of what your life will look like should you embody your true nature and step into your purpose. The vision requires a great deal of awareness if you are to notice it when it flashes into your mind's eye.

Even if it presents itself multiple times over, the person too distracted by the many cares of this world will never see it. Recognizing it requires a certain stillness. It demands an emptying of the mind of the effervescent and elusive desire for pleasures and escapism that keep our attention in a trap. The vision will need to be clarified. It won't present with 100% certainty. It will be vague.

Frequently, when an open heart is exposed to Truth, that very Truth is the trigger needed for the vision to present itself. This is one of the reasons why your environment is so important. If you are constantly exposed to lies, it will be a tall task to discover the Truth. But when the people around you live off of the established laws of God that govern our world, it opens your spiritual eyes and enhances your vision.

This is because Truth is also Light. When there is no vision, it is because you are surrounded by darkness. Where the Truth is, Light is also there, illuminating the room. Vision isn't some esoteric tool available only to those who engage in sorcery. Quite the contrary. Vision is simply the mind's eye being receptive to Truth. The Light that accompanies Truth is what allows you to see your vision.

Thoughts are one of the most powerful tools on this planet. When your mind is opened up, it allows you to have higher thoughts. And there will be a specific set of thoughts that create an image in your mind that creates an imprint of hope onto your spirit. This image will never leave you. It will constantly agitate your spirit in some way.

The image will create intense joy and peace if you have enough courage to pursue it. But the further you move away from it, the more regret and shame you will feel when the image is brought to the front of your mind. That image is your vision. That image will never leave you. This is another characteristic of your vision. It will never leave you.

It is your responsibility and privilege to give the vision detail. You must insert people with faces and names, buildings, streets, colors, and every detail you can conjure up. The more detail you give to your vision, the stronger it will be. When you have an extremely detailed vision, you can do anything. This is because the more detail *you give* to your vision, the greater your capacity for faith in your vision becomes.

But what is Faith? Faith is being certain of what you hope for and convinced of what you cannot *see*. There is a distinct correlation between what you can see with your eyes open versus what you can see with your eyes closed. Within your imagination, what you can see is unlimited. With your eyes, what you can see is limited.

How can you be certain of a *hope*? You can't see a hope. You can't touch a hope. And the only reason you hope for something is because you don't have the object of what you hope for. Even more so, how can you be convinced of something you cannot see?

The answer lies within the details. When you give details to your vision, it becomes real to you. It can only exist in the physical realm after it's given details. It needs to have size, shape, color, names, symbols, substance, texture, location, boundaries, intent, etc. *The details you provide become the blueprint for your vision.*

One aspect that all blueprints have is documentation. You need to get the vision on paper or some form of documentation. Then, you must continue adding as many details as possible until it becomes as realistic as the objects you can see around you. Draw it out if you can. If you can't draw, ask someone who can draw to give your vision life. Doing this will make the imprint of your vision upon your heart even more potent. This *deep* imprint will create something called crazy faith. A deep level of conviction and hope that surpasses logic.

Crazy Faith

I only saw my dad cry on two occasions. The first time, he and my mom were going through turmoil in their marriage. The second time he cried, I was around ten years old. I'll never forget it. It was time to take my weekend trip to my dad's house. Only this day, my dad had a nasty headache. He always had headaches, though, so I didn't think anything of it.

As I watched television in the living room, I could hear sobbing coming from the bathroom. Struck with curiosity, I walked over to the bathroom to see my dad crying on the floor. Jenn, his girlfriend, stood over him, asking if he was okay. He kept saying he was fine, but Jenn knew better than to listen to his pride. My dad hated having to go to the hospital. What happened next was a blur.

Jenn rushed me and my siblings to change clothes because we were heading to the hospital. But she dropped me and my sister off at the community center on the way to the hospital. I assume Jenn didn't want us to see whatever happened next. After some time, she returned to get us, and naturally, she took us to the hospital to see my dad.

On the way, she started explaining what the doctor told her. He had a tumor in his brain that was crushing his pituitary gland. He had to be rushed into an Operating Room to have the doctors remove the tumor. The surgery went well, but we couldn't see him until he woke up. I distinctly remember this conversation, but I don't remember feeling particularly hurt as she was explaining all this to me with tears running down her face.

It wasn't until we got to the hospital that it hit me. As we walked into the waiting room, I saw a lot of familiar faces. My aunt, uncles, grandma, and other siblings were all there. Shortly after, my mom even showed up. After a while, I remember a nurse telling us that he had woken up, and we could see him in the intensive care unit. She warned us that he may not be all the way there due to the anesthetic.

As we all walked in and gathered around him, he was shaking terribly. He kept saying to the nurse that he was cold. He could barely speak, and he looked slightly confused. After seeing him like that, I broke. I immediately started crying. Looking around the room, I noticed I wasn't alone in my despair. Everyone was crying except for one person: my grandma.

She stood there as joyous as if she'd won the lottery. I was utterly puzzled. How could she see her son like that and be so happy? She was completely unbothered. I thought she was crazy! But years later, she and I were having one of our long talks. We reminisced about that day, recalling the details of our story.

From my perspective, I told her the story and why I thought she was crazy. I just had to know why she was so unbothered by it. Her answer blew me away! She looked at me with a cigarette between her pointer and middle finger and said, "Jake! I knew yo daddy was gone be alright! I knew he was destined to do great things ever since he was a little boy. He had just gotten started building his legacy and maturing. I knew it wasn't his time yet. Not until he left his mark." My grandma had so much faith in the vision she saw for my dad that even as he lay on what seemed to me to be his deathbed, she knew that wasn't his reality. How crazy is that?!

She had such a detailed vision of his life that anything that showed up in this three-dimensional space that didn't match her vision she didn't accept as reality. She only had faith in the vision that lived in her mind. So much so that even as her son faced death, she only saw and acted in accord with what she saw in her imagination. So much so that when I saw her actions, I thought, "Granny is crazy!" *That* is crazy faith.

A detailed vision creates something called *crazy faith*. What is crazy faith? It's when you are so convinced of the reality of something that only exists in your imagination that you begin to live as if you can see it with your physical eyes. It is when you act like something exists in the physical world even though nobody else can *see* it. When other people notice your faith, they begin to think that you are crazy! When you start acting as if something is real, your faith exponentially increases the probability of it eventually becoming real.

We've given this phenomenon several names. Some people call it a *self-fulfilling prophecy*. Recently, it's been called the *law of attraction*. Napoleon Hill coined the phrase *autosuggestion* to describe the trait. Earl Nightingale called it *The Strangest Secret*.

I like to call it *crazy faith*. Consistent thoughts will manifest within your identity. They leave a mark on your belief system. That belief will start showing up in your life before the vision breaks through the soil. When that happens, people will start to give you the *side-eye*. This is a good thing. It means you are on the right path. It represents the fact that your vision is authentic. No true vision will come to fruition without meeting some form of difficulty.

Plan

Lastly is the plan. You have a compass (mission) and a map (vision). Now, all you have to do is choose a path. The plan is a model of the path you believe will accomplish the mission. After you've created a *blueprint* of the vision, you can get to work on your plan. This is why I stated in one of the principles, "Purpose is the foundation of all plans." To plan without purpose is to purposely fail.

You have to go to that vision 5,10,20,40 years down the line and reverse engineer it to where you are now. I like to call this bringing the future into the present moment. If you do this, no matter what happens in your present reality, you will be on a path towards your envisioned reality. People who act according to their present reality are walking by sight. But people who act according to their imagined reality are walking by faith.

Some people won't start without a plan. Others don't even want to think about a plan. Is a plan mandatory? No. Is a plan beneficial? Yes! Life is complicated, and we need every piece of leverage we can get. After you plan, there is a strong tendency to become attached to the plan. You must realize that the plan is merely a means of getting you off to the best start possible.

A plan is *not* intended to map out your every move so that you know every step. Because we cannot see the future, knowing *every* step before it's taken is impossible. Things will always go differently than the way you plan it. This is why you must detach yourself from the plan after it is created.

You may be thinking, "Why, in the name of orange juice jones, would I create and follow a plan that I know won't come to fruition? Why do I need a plan that I can't count on?" From the surface, creating and following a plan may seem counterintuitive. Let me explain a little further. There are two *critical* reasons for having a plan.

A plan is the starting block for your journey. You don't need to have a plan to start. You do need to have a plan if you want to be able to get off to the best start possible. This is similar to why sprinters begin their race with starting blocks. They provide acceleration and traction at the beginning of the race, so you have a better start. That's one of the *critical* reasons for having a plan: a better start.

Adaptability is crucial because it's what gets you to the finish line. However, adaptability is extremely difficult. It's one of the hardest things ever. Adaptability requires you to be willing to do whatever is needed at that moment to stay on track toward completion. Sometimes, you'll have to be demanding. Other times, you will have to be confrontational. Or, you may need to be patient. Still, some situations will require you to be willing to stand out in the cold. Other times, you'll have to be willing to stand out in the heat.

Here is the bottom line. You have to be willing to do whatever it takes. That's what adaptability is. The reason this is difficult is that we have our preferences. To adapt, you have to go against your preferences. You must go against what you'd typically do. Some areas in life make us feel comfortable, and the mind does everything it can to keep us in an area of comfort. When a situation requires someone to get uncomfortable, 95% of the people in the world will be unwilling to *do whatever it takes.*

The *average* person is not willing to adapt to accomplish the mission. This is another reason why the Bruce Lee quote, "You must be like water," that I've mentioned before, is essential. Water can adapt to whatever shape it needs to. Even though this is a tall order, it is a trait that will accomplish the mission. The second *key* reason for planning is adaptability.

Since planning is variable, you can't plan once and be done. A part of adapting is replanning. Very much like a GPS system will reroute when a new direction is taken. A new plan is made to make sure the mission is accomplished. That's why every organization that has been successful in the marketplace has two components in their planning: Persistence and frequency.

They never plan and then attach to that plan, hoping everything works out. They set their mission, detail a vision, and create a plan. Afterward, their focus shifts to acting out the plan and adapting it to what happens in the real world. Then, they reconvene, replan, *act, and adapt* for a set period.

It becomes a never-ending cycle of planning, action, and adapting to whatever is thrown their way. But it's also a cycle with a purpose. The plan will get you out of the blocks and ahead of the field. But adaptability will get you to the result.

The point of the plan is to get you moving toward the vision. The point of the vision is to give you something to put faith in until the mission is brought to fruition. When the mission is realized, the purpose is personified. The purpose is always for you to become. Once you become, you'll start to do things differently and then begin to have different things. Once you become, you'll activate the be-do-have sequence in the proper order. *This entire process is your "good work."*

The work that has been prepared for you beforehand. It's all inside of you. You merely have to pull it out. God brought Adam into the world to work. He brought you into the world to work. This is your work. As my good friend Myron Golden says, all work works.

You may not believe the work works because you have yet to get your desired outcome. That's because the work is working on you. It's working on you to turn you into the person you were meant to become. Once you become the person that can do the work, the work will work for you.

This is the *other side of the coin.* On the one side, the work works *on you.* On the other side, the work works *for you.* Everyone wants the work to work for them, but they have yet to become the person that the work can work for. Talk about a tongue twister. So, by God's design, the work has to work on them.

If you can tolerate the work that the work does on you until you become the person that the work can work for, you will get to enjoy the other side of the coin. Once it's flipped, you can only fully see the other side of the coin. That's another reason why many people believe their purpose changes. They set out to accomplish what they believe to be their purpose, only to quit once the work goes to work on making them become a better person. But remember, purpose never changes. Only we do.

There is a static nature to the mission and the purpose. Those two will not change. In contrast, the vision and the plan are variable. These two can and will change. Because the vision is merely a snapshot of a much larger whole, there can be multiple visions that represent different points in time. One can be fulfilled, and another will appear. Likewise, plans will also change. Change is one of the things that is permanent in this world. It is a characteristic of time that things within its dimension must change. As the circumstances around us change, our plans must change if the mission is to be realized. Because the mission is tied to purpose, it must always stay constant.

To fully understand your mission, vision, and plan, you have to be willing to sit with yourself for some time. Just like with purpose, you must do the inner work to develop the tools to pull this out. However, this is the establishment of you discovering what direction your life should be going in. So, it is well worth the time.

Everything we have discussed in this book is internal work. You don't need anything other than a willing spirit and patience to reveal all this information about your true self. You may be thinking, "How can I have confidence that all of this is my *true* purpose in life?" In the book's last section, we will discuss what I call The Filtration System. It is a series of questions to give you the confidence you need in the inner work you've done to propel you forward.

> **Coach's Challenge:** How far out can you go? Can you go 100 years into the future and decide what you want to see? One generation is roughly 25 years. How can you impact the next four generations in your family? What can you do in each of the Core 5 that can help your loved ones in the critical subdomains of their life even after you have left this Earth? What about 75 years from now? What about 50 years from now? What about 25, 10, even 5 years from now?
>
> I call this the "100-year life plan"! The goal isn't to try to predict what will happen in these timeframes. But what do you envision for your Core 5? This exercise will make you think in a way you may have never done before. This is not something to be done in one day. It will take lots of time and deep thinking. Give it some time, and keep coming back to it. It will be worth it in the end.

Chapter 7 Summary:

- Nobody builds a home without first creating a blueprint. Truthfully, no building is built without first building blueprints. In creating the building of your life, you must first draw out your blueprint. You've already got the most critical piece...your purpose. This serves as the foundation of your life.

- But no building is complete with only a foundation. A foundation is meant to be built upon. The external structure must be built. This is your mission. Your mission is created when your purpose is attached to the people you were meant to serve. Your mission offers your life direction and becomes a compass. Your mission is your tool of transformation.

- When you have your mission, you can also write out your *life purpose statement: The Purpose for my life is to* **be** *a(n)* _____ *(your dharma) for* _____ *(your people)*

- Your vision is a snapshot of what your life will look like when you embody your purpose. The more detail you add to your vision, the more powerful your faith will be. Even to the point of crazy faith: the unwavering conviction in the reality of something existing in one's imagination, even when others may perceive it as irrational.

- The last part of your building is the internal furnishings. This is the plan for your life. Having a mission (compass) and a vision (map) is essential, but the plan is the model of the path chosen to achieve the mission. Your vision needs to be reverse-engineered, bringing the future into the present moment. In turn, you must act based on your imagined reality rather than your present circumstances.

The mission, vision, and plan all work together to support purpose. While the vision and plan are subject to change and need adaptability from us, purpose is static and requires commitment and endurance.

CHAPTER 8

THE FILTER:

How To Be Confident In The Purpose You Discover And Pursue

F iltration systems have been around for quite some time. They are used in conjunction with several things. But filters are most often associated with water. The intention behind using a filter is to remove any contaminants from polluting a substance or system.

It's a reasonably substantial little piece of equipment. Consider what the removal of a filter would mean for any water system. In that circumstance, it will definitely reduce and eventually cease the entire system.

When referencing purpose in life, multiple pollutants could enter the *river of purpose* and destroy its purity. There is a filtration system that anyone can use to be sure the purpose you pursue is free from contaminants. The filter ensures that what you see as your purpose in life is in line with your true nature and eternal purpose.

What if you lived your entire life living a lie? What if, one day, you discovered that everything you have pursued was a complete waste of time? Would it not be a waste of your life to think you have been living on purpose only to find out once it's too late that you've been wrong all along? That would be a tragedy. Most people don't sit down to gain clarity and alignment concerning the direction of their lives.

That is why I came up with the filtration system. It is meant to be a series of questions that will reveal anything that does not belong on your journey. This way, you can have confidence that the direction you are traveling in is tailored for you. The last thing you want to do is waste your life pursuing a mirage.

This is one of the biggest concerns with revealing your Ikigai (your reason for being). What if you throw your entire life at an aim, and it turns out to be a waste? The filter gives you the confidence to know your aim isn't off.

Please understand that this doesn't mean everything will always be *easy peasy*. There is no guarantee that everything will be easy. As a matter of fact, it is more of a guarantee that there will be affliction. Many are the afflictions of the righteous. When you are on the right path, you can bet your bottom dollar it won't be easy. But you can also bet your bottom dollar it will be worth your while.

Additionally, I want to make a point while the conversation leads in this direction. Many people believe that their purpose in life will be the most notable victory of their life. In essence, it will be. But beneath the surface, it will often also be accompanied by sacrifice. The victory that comes from purpose will often be tied to sacrifice.

You have to sacrifice your time and your desires. Sometimes, your purpose may require you to loosen ties with loved ones. The severity of sacrifice will be different for everyone. However, there will be some form of sacrifice needed. The most prominent sacrifice is the one of your current Self. To become who you were created to become, you have to remove who you currently are. You can't be two people. You have to sacrifice one for the other. Either sacrifice the eternal Self and continue as you are or sacrifice the temporary Self and transform.

Use the filtration system to ensure the purpose you have revealed is *aligned* with your true purpose. How can you distinguish the purpose you've revealed from your *actual* purpose? How do you know that this is the purpose that was designed for you? That is what the filtration system is. Alignment is a huge part of ensuring you have the confidence to move forward.

Filtering Impurities

When we talk about alignment, we are referencing coordination between the purpose The Creator prepared for you before you were born and the purpose you use as the foundation for your life's Mission, Vision, and Plan. This implies that it's possible to miss the mark and have wasted a lifetime.

The fact is that we were all brought here with purpose. However, we were also given free will. Therefore, nobody is forced to pursue and realize purpose in their life. I've mentioned it before, but everyone has to choose between life and death. The two have been laid at our feet, and every decision we make comes from one of the two.

There are different aspects of alignment to be aware of. There is alignment between The Creator's intentions and our own intentions. Then, there is also alignment between your purpose's components (Time, People, and Identity). Lastly, there must be alignment between your purpose, mission, vision, and plan. When it comes to alignment with The Creator's intentions and our own, a specific set of questions will filter out any unwanted contaminants. The alignment of the components will ensure they all align with your eternal purpose.

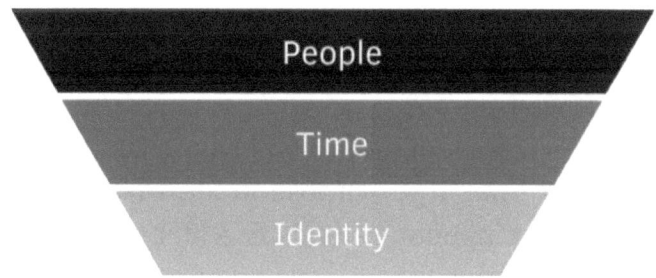

The first part of the filtration system is used to examine all that you've mapped out in this phase. Everything you've revealed about your purpose will be looked at. I've mentioned all these components at the beginning of the book. However, you must revisit them as a part of the filtration system. Having gone through all the material, you can look at these components from a completely different lens.

People

The first part of the filter is People. Who does your purpose affect? Is it solely or even primarily focused on Self? There needs to be a nation or a tribe of people that your purpose is connected to. No one's *true* purpose in life will be selfish in nature.

Even if the number of people you have the influence to touch *right now* seems small, others with similar values, beliefs, and vision are available worldwide. The *others* are available for your influence to tap into as you grow and step into your purpose.

If what you have as your purpose doesn't meet this, I'd suggest that you use this piece of the filter and go back to the drawing board. Continue to visit the tools of revelation and enjoy the process of getting to know yourself better.

Time

The second part of the filter is time. Regarding all the components of your purpose you've constructed, how long will the impact be felt? Is it something that will have a lasting change? Will it be short-lived? Your true purpose in life will be attached to a timeline that, at a minimum, extends to a lifetime. If your purpose doesn't meet the criteria for this portion of the filter, I'd utilize the filter and revisit the tools mentioned in earlier sections.

Identity

The third part of the filter is the element of identity. Throughout this book, I've been saying your purpose is not something you do. It definitely isn't something that you have. Your purpose in life is who you are supposed to be. Everything else comes from you becoming the person you were meant to be.

Becoming is not something that is accomplished. Identity is meant to be embodied. That embodiment is then to be sustained for the duration of your existence. Your purpose is not meant to be a moment of accomplishment along the spectrum of time. It is meant to be your *true* identity that you will embody for this lifetime and beyond.

Your accomplishments and your possessions are left behind. But your identity is attached to your spirit, which lives forever. If your purpose is <u>not</u> tied to who you are supposed to become, you may need to revisit the tools. Remember, your purpose is eternal, so its components must also be eternal. You cannot take what you do or what you have, set it in the place of purpose, and expect it to function correctly.

After using the above three filters, you can check for alignment between your purpose, mission, vision, and plan. Be sure your plan isn't entirely off course from your true identity. Your vision should be similar to your mission, and so on. When these four align, your life will also be in alignment.

Filtering Misalignment

This portion of the filter is used to gain alignment with your *true* purpose to ensure your life isn't wasted on something that wasn't meant for you. The system is a series of questions you can ask yourself that will filter out unwanted beliefs, notions, and outside influences from polluting your life's purpose.

Question #1 - Is my purpose consistent with Truth?

There is a massive prerequisite here. That is, one must know what Truth is. What is Truth?! Truth is the natural order of things. The systems that have been set up by God that govern our world. The Truth about love, life, friendship, servitude, faith, forgiveness, peace, etc.

For example, one Truth is the Truth of cause & effect. Some people call it Karma. This is a Spiritual Truth. You will always reap what you sow. If you sow discord, you will reap discord. If you sow love, you will reap love. If you sow destruction, you reap destruction. Plant more of what you want out of life. This Truth applies to any and every aspect of life.

A second and probably more known example is one of the Truths of relationship, "Love your neighbor as yourself." Spiritual Truths exist, and your purpose in life would never be contrary to these Truths. If what you see as your *true* purpose violates a Spiritual Truth, it is not your *true* purpose.

Question #2 - Do I have genuine peace about the purpose I've revealed?

When you are aligned with your true purpose, a distinct calmness will fall over your spirit. An inexplicable peace will take over your mind. There will be no doubt. Instead, you will be full of faith. Often, it is a certainty that you may not be able to explain.

This is sometimes referred to as instinct. A deep conviction that lacks logical explanation. You're convinced that it's real, but you can't confidently provide any evidence that others would deem substantial. The only thing you have to show for it is faith.

I attended a conference in Charlotte, North Carolina, a few years ago. I had never been there before. I stayed for a week in the downtown area. I went with a few of my co-workers. One of whom was from Maryland and was familiar with the area. He also had a few friends who moved to the Charlotte area. They were having dinner, and he invited me out with them, so I tagged along.

We went to this soul food restaurant that was amazing. One of the guys eating with us burst into tears as we ate dinner. I was utterly taken aback by his tears because they were so random. Luckily, he immediately began to explain himself before the rest of us could get the shocked and confused look off our faces.

He went into a story about how his mother had died a few weeks earlier. Apparently, the song that came on inside the restaurant was her favorite song. The song was the only stimulus he needed for the waterworks to start flowing. He said he had been trying to avoid hearing it since she passed. The conversation continued, and eventually, we got to the topic of his work. He talked about his commute, which part of town he lived in, and why.

After we left, my co-worker explained how close they used to be when they were younger. We went to a comedy show the next day after the conference activities concluded. On the final day, I attended a baseball game and went to an outlet mall. Nothing extraordinary. But I remember a pivotal moment at the outlet mall very vividly.

There was a waterfall near the center of the mall. I went and sat on the waterfall and called my family. I showed them what the mall looked like through the video call, and then we ended the call.

As I hung up the phone, I had this deep conviction telling me this was the area I needed to live. I couldn't explain why then, and I can't explain it now. But without any doubt, I knew that I was supposed to be there. I plan on moving there after my current enlistment is up. Lord willing, I'll be able to write about it in my next book and have some grandiose story to go along with it.

We may have moments of desire that are similar to this. Although, they are often accompanied by intense questioning and doubt. Some decisions in life will keep you awake at night. They will bother your mind with endless anxieties and worries. You should always pay attention to this. If your life's purpose presents itself this way, you must filter it out and revisit the tools.

If a thought is bothering you in a reoccurring way for any reason, examine yourself to discover the reason and adjust accordingly. Consider that nerve-rattling feeling a gift from God, a sign telling you to re-route. It won't be like this with your true and eternal purpose. It'll come with peace and confidence, even amid uncertainty.

Question #3 - Will my purpose result in unrest and regret for the rest of my life?

Many emotions come with unrest and regret. Guilt and shame are the two that are most prominent. If anybody is found guilty, trouble always follows! If the judge finds someone to be guilty, they are sentenced to prison. The last thing you want is guilt. Shame isn't any better. Engaging in shameful acts wreaks havoc upon your mind.

Caught in a spiral of embarrassment, you often become your worst critic. Guilt is often associated with unlawful acts. Shame is closely linked with immoral acts. Closely related to the above filter, that feeling of uneasiness before you make a momentous decision explodes with a gamut of emotions and thoughts that are toxic to your well-being if ignored.

You then have a feeling of regret for the rest of your life, usually accompanied by a strong case of the "should of, could of, would ofs." If you feel anything similar to this concerning your purpose in life, it is not your <u>true</u> purpose.

Question #4 - Can I expect God to be pleased with who I am becoming?

The phrasing behind this question is very intentional. This is a question that deserves much meditation and dedicated time. If you do not believe in God, I urge you to just go with it. If you are not sold about Him, just make-believe for a moment. Nobody has to know about this except you. Let your mind run free. Humor me for the sake of your life and everyone who is counting on your true purpose to shine through you.

Would God, in all of his wisdom, splendor, and power be pleased with who you are on the road to becoming? The identity that you have revealed for the purpose of your life. The mission and vision you've revealed. If you had the opportunity and honor to stand before God at this very moment and present him with all that you've just revealed about your life, would he be pleased?

Don't let the algorithm of your heart steal this moment. Stay right here in the pages of this book. Block out everything and everyone else. It's you and God. As you sit together, you tell him all that you've uncovered. What does he say? Is he delighted? Maybe he responds with a grin? What is his initial response? Let the theatre of your imagination play its images and simply observe. Maybe he gives you additional insights? Maybe he is disgusted? Would he open his Word and show you a scripture? What scripture would He take you to?

This question may be challenging to answer. The difficulty only exists in the emotions and beliefs that block your imagination. Again, I urge you to just open your mind and see what's in there. The answer will come to you.

As this chapter comes to a close, we will close out the book with a quick summary of everything discussed in the book.

Chapter 8 Summary:

- The Filter was designed to ensure that one's pursued purpose aligns with one's true nature and eternal purpose. Having alignment underscores the importance of ensuring that the identified purpose is in harmony with the individual's true calling.

- The Filter is a series of questions designed to give you clarity and confidence that the purpose you've revealed is aligned with your true purpose. Here's a quick snapshot:

  - Filtering Impurities:

    - People: Who does your purpose affect? Is it solely or even primarily focused on Self?

    - Time: Is it something that will have a lasting change? Will it be short-lived?

    - Identity: Is your revealed purpose something to become, something to do, or something to have?

  - Filtering Misalignment:

    - Is my purpose consistent with Truth?

    - Do I have genuine peace about the purpose I've revealed?

    - Will my purpose result in unrest and regret for the rest of my life?

    - Can I expect God to be pleased with who I am becoming?

Conclusion

M eet John and Doe. They are identical twins. John knows his life's purpose and lives in it every day. Doe doesn't know his life's purpose. Who has a higher probability of living longer, healthier, and wealthier? The studies tell us John has Doe beat by an astounding 240%. I hope you've been picking up what I've been putting down. Your purpose is the key to the life you've been dreaming of. Our Creator has placed it inside of you to further His plans. Let's take a trip down memory lane and revisit all the concepts discussed.

In phase one, we discussed the five principles that will guarantee success in this framework and in life.

Chapter 1: The Principles – Adopting the *purpose mindset* is vital in anyone's journey toward purpose. In the chapter, we discussed the five principles that need to be adopted as beliefs to guarantee success. Here are the five immutable principles: 1) Everything and Everyone Has a Purpose, 2) Purpose is Internal, 3) We're Already Equipped for Purpose, 4) Purpose is The Foundation of Plans, and 5) The Purpose of All Mankind is To Serve.

All five of these principles are assets that need to be added to your mindset. Recall that your mindset can be an asset or a liability. Owning a mindset that is a liability will cause a life opposed to the Truth.

In phase two, we began to discuss the underlying concepts around purpose. Phase two revealed why you need to know your purpose, what your purpose can do for you, and how your view of your purpose affects your life.

Chapter 2: The Prescription – Your life's purpose is like a magic pill that provides countless benefits. It promises improvements in longevity, memory, sleep, decision-making, problem-solving, reasoning, overall health, financial well-being, and emotional states. Side effects include joy, peace, and resilience. And this is just the tip of the iceberg. All you have to do is choose to take it... *every day*!

Chapter 3: The Pathways – There's nothing as peaceful as an ice-cold bucket of water to the face to wake you up. Triggers are always going off, trying to wake you up from your sleep. Anybody who chooses to stop living among the walking dead and step into purpose does so on one of the three pathways to purpose: 1) Reactive Pathway, 2) Proactive Pathway, or 3) Interactive Pathway.

Chapter 4: The Perspectives – Does Obstruction, Observation, or Obscurity best describe who you are? Obstruction is divided into four neighborhoods or precincts: The Dark, Property, Immediacy, and Self. Obscurity consists of four precincts: The Fog, Activity, Lifetime, and Others. And, of course, the capital, Observation, has four: The Light, Identity, Eternal, and Humanity.

Which pair of lenses have you been walking through life with? Do you wear a blindfold, prescription glasses, or drunk goggles? We don't view life as it is, but how we perceive it to be. That is why this chapter is so important. Understanding what our current perspective is and how it impacts us is enormous. It becomes nearly impossible to change perspective if you don't know your current one is broken.

Chapter 5: The Potential – There are two purposes that everyone should be concerned with. First is their *current* purpose. Second is their *true* purpose. This chapter was designed to help you identify your *current* purpose. Additionally, your *current* purpose may be limiting your potential in your Core 5: 1) Faith, 2) Fellowship, 3) Fitness, 4) Finance, and 5) Fruitfulness.

Closing the gap between your *current* and *true* purpose is how you tap into unlimited potential. It also solidifies your predestined position as a sovereign ruler in your domain. It is your responsibility and privilege to establish your position within your domain. When you do, you'll unlock the same for several others. Some of which you may not even be aware your influence touched.

Chapter 6: The Revelation – This chapter discusses the big revelation. Your purpose is an identity that you embody and personify. Where your compassions, passions, and expertise have commonalities, your purpose is revealed. Your gifts, calling, and value can also be revealed. Through the Tools of Revelation, you can identify your beliefs, ideas, and thoughts that reveal your purpose.

Chapter 7: The Blueprint – After you've revealed your purpose, you must build your mission. This is the fun part. At this stage, you get to solve the purpose equation ($P4P=1/P+P$), add as much detail as possible to your vision, develop crazy faith, and plan out your future. Lastly, you get to create a *life purpose statement: The Purpose for my life is to **be** a(n) _____ (your dharma) for _____ (your people).*

Creating your blueprint is the process of building around your purpose. It's a critical step in giving your life the direction and clarity you desire and deserve.

Chapter 8: The Filter – Now that you know your true purpose, how can you have conviction in what you've revealed? Are you 100% certain that it's accurate? This is the reason I created the filter. To align God's purpose for your life and the purpose you've revealed through this process.

What's Next?

I never thought I would be able to write a book. I always knew I could write, but I hated writing my papers and reports in high school, so I always told myself that I didn't like writing. My mindset shifted when I started discovering who I am and what I can do.

Through my self-discovery process, I slowly unveiled who I truly am. The next thing I knew, I found myself writing an accountability contract with my uncle, saying I'd have a book written within the next 90 days or else I'd pay him $1,000. Not only that, but I'd also owe him $100 every month after that until the book was written. I got it done in 30 days. I tell that story to say that you don't really know what you are capable of. There's more in you than you believe.

I hope this book was of extreme value to you. We covered all three phases of the process: Mindset, Understanding Purpose, and Revealing Purpose. It's quite a bit of information. Also, I know that not everyone will successfully complete the exercises the first time.

I know this because I didn't successfully go through them the first time. I had to go back and utilize the tools of revelation for a few months before trying the exercises again. I spent ample time ruminating over everything I was learning about and meditating upon the new discoveries about myself.

The second time, I entered the exercises equipped with enough ammunition to take out a small army! It was around 3 am, and it took me around 20 minutes to clarify my purpose. It took me hours the first time, and I felt extremely uncomfortable and unclear afterward. The principles and concepts in this book will work for you as long as you work them.

This book is the first in a series of three. After digesting all this material, you may think, "What now?" This is certainly how I felt after I had my discovery. I immediately began putting my blueprint to work so I could step into my purpose in life. However, I noticed that the more I attempted to step into who I am meant to be, I felt like I was trying to run through a brick wall.

Revealing your purpose in life is the easy part. Going through the process of embodying that identity is an entirely different beast. It's not easy to become a new and improved you when the current you is all you have ever known. It takes a bigger mindset to adopt an entirely new set of principles and step into your purpose.

That's what the second book will be about. It will be a step-by-step process to take everything you've revealed in this book and get through all the boundaries preventing you from stepping into your purpose. I believe that book will be just as, if not more, powerful as this one. The third and final book will be a guide. It will be for those who want to reach out and help others go through the process I've revealed in the first two books.

I am here to serve you by restoring order in your life. I hope to do that through this material and all the other content I have in the works. Remember that you were brought here for a reason! Now that you know what it is, grab it by the handle and hop along for the ride. God Bless!

Until Next Time,

Jaye Purpose

P.S. If you want more help with your purpose or bringing a purpose-centered culture into your business, contact us at www.thepurposepad.com. You will find several resources and tools to help you along your journey!

Works Cited

[1]Ackerman, C. (2021). 28 Benefits of Gratitude & Most Significant Research Findings. *Positive Psychology*. Retrieved from https://positivepsychology.com/benefits-gratitude-research-questions/

[2]Ahmad FB, Anderson RN. The Leading Causes of Death in the US for 2020. JAMA. 2021;325(18):1829–1830. doi:10.1001/jama.2021.5469

[3]Alimujiang A, Wiensch A, Boss J, et al. Association Between Life Purpose and Mortality Among US Adults Older Than 50 Years. JAMA *Netw Open*. 2019;2(5):e194270. doi:10.1001/jamanetworkopen.2019.4270

[4]Bates & Gallup. (2019). *Forging Pathways to Purposeful Work: The Role of Higher Education*. Forging Pathways to Purposeful Work: The Role of Higher Education - Gallup

[5]Bravery, K. (2018). People first: Mercer's 2018 Global Talent Trends Study People first: Mercer's 2018 Global Talent Trends Study | Mercer.

[6]Csikszentmihalyi, M. (2008). Flow: The psychology of optimal experience. New York: Harper Perennial.

[7]Hill, P. L., & Turiano, N. A. (2014). Purpose in Life as a Predictor of Mortality Across Adulthood. Psychological Science, 25(7), 1482–1486. https://doi.org/10.1177/0956797614531799

[8]Kantar. (2020). Purpose 2020: The Journey Towards Purpose Led-Growth. Purpose 2020 (kantar.com)

[9]Nathan A. Lewis, Nicholas A. Turiano, Brennan R. Payne & Patrick L. Hill (2017) Purpose in life and cognitive functioning in adulthood, Aging, Neuropsychology, and Cognition, 24:6, 662-671, DOI: 10.1080/13825585.2016.1251549

[10]Novelli, P. (2020). Executive Purpose Study. Porter Novelli Executive Purpose Study: Leadership, Action & Accountability at the C-suite - Porter Novelli

[11]Sisodia, R. (2014). 2nd Edition, Firms of Endearment: How World Class Companies Profit From Passion and Purpose. Firms of Endearment | Second Edition

[12]Suzanne Hidi & K. Ann Renninger (2006) The Four-Phase Model of Interest Development, Educational Psychologist, 41:2, 111-127, DOI: 10.1207/s15326985ep4102_4

[13]Tseng, J., Poppenk, J. Brain meta-state transitions demarcate thoughts across task contexts exposing the mental noise of trait neuroticism. *Nat Commun* **11,** 3480 (2020). https://doi.org/10.1038/s41467-020-17255-9

[14]Turner et al. Sleep Science and Practice (2017) 1:14 DOI 10.1186/s41606-017-0015-6

www.ingramcontent.com/pod-product-compliance
Lightning Source LLC
Chambersburg PA
CBHW020446130626
46549CB00001B/314